Arguments for Our Competitive Emotions

Arguments for Our Competitive Emotions

How We Express Ourselves

Russell A. Konkel

VANTAGE PRESS
New York

Published by Vantage Press, Inc.
516 West 34th Street, New York, New York 10001

Manufactured in the United States of America
ISBN: 0-533-11254-0

Library of Congress Catalog Card No.: 94-90477

0 9 8 7 6 5 4 3 2 1

To those interested in relaxing their emotions

Contents

Introduction

Many books and articles have been written about man's competitiveness. Some say: "Man is naturally competitive," while others say: "Everything man does is competitive." Still we don't utilize this. Our mental health field doesn't recognize that competitiveness is important for man's emotional stability. This book will illustrate, I hope, that man should not ignore his competitive nature but be able to understand its importance in our mental well-being. More knowledge about the emotions will lead to more understanding of how we can fulfill our emotional needs.

Arguments for Our Competitive Emotions

1

The Competitive Emotions

I believe, and it seems obvious, that man is naturally competitive. If so, this assumption must have application in the field of mental health.

For the past thirty years I have worked directly with disturbed and mentally ill people in institutional settings and in my own group home. Since working with these people in the institutional setting and having read books on mental health, I have found books to be basically lacking. In other words, I could not apply this information and get it to do the job of mental rehabilitation. I finally started to realize that the mental health area was missing something and over the years have decided what some of these missing elements are. It was like having all the parts of a puzzle but trying to put them together in the wrong way. It must be very frustrating and dissatisfying to people who are working directly with mental patients in institutions today when the information they use does not accomplish what it should. Our mental health field is not doing the best job, and mental illness is growing at an alarming rate. People need to realize this and start exploring ways to improve the system so that it becomes more effective.

I have extensive experience working directly with people with emotional difficulties. Most people with mental problems are failure-oriented; this means they do not feel as though they are capable of winning, only losing. Giving them only rest and the least restrictive environment, as a therapist would recommend, and not getting them to interact competitively ignores this basic block or treats it as semiunimportant. Treating their lack of competition should be considered first, as they probably have had too much rest already and do not need any more time reflecting on their failures. The major component of mental health should be to get a person to compete, not in the least restrictive environment, but in the most competitive, interactive environment possible under the circumstances.

I have over thirty years of working directly with people with mental difficulties in institutions and in my own group home settings, and I'm interested in people who view the mind as I do and would like to discuss these observations and come up with some better ideas. So I'll present my views simply.

I won't go into how I view emotional imagery or innate and subconscious behavior, just what seems necessary to get enough satisfaction in our minds to be able to operate in a somewhat normal fashion and feel fairly comfortable. I am not a scholar and am not writing about complicated mental problems, only those that we can see easily and clearly understand.

Man may, in his ever-changing environment, try new ideas or concepts that happen to come along. He strives to achieve these ideas as goals because of his competitive energies. Making these goals compatible with the rest of his emotions is what he has to do. If he can't make these ever-changing goals of his environment compatible with his innate emotions, he will have emotional troubles, for his innate emotional knowledge will not change.

Since the release of competitive emotions is intriguing because of their effect on our lives, we wonder what their importance is to our existence. Are they a by-product of our emotions? If so, why does the brain demand such a constant need for the release of these energies, and why are they involved constantly in so much of our lives? Perhaps we should attempt to see how they are used in our lives to see whether we should think about them and try to understand them.

Competitive energy needs to be released by the individual in order for that individual to be mentally healthy. The less a person is able to release these energies, the more depressed a person becomes and the less normal he or she will be in relationships with others. Show me a person who is able to release his or her competitive energies and you will see a happy, somewhat normal person, even if he or she has other problems.

Some emotional feelings of success must accompany competitiveness. These feelings of success are not always obvious.

I propose that the normal release of competitive energies is necessary for a healthy individual. Abnormal release of pent-up energy shows up in individuals in anger, and if this energy is not released, then it results in anxiety and depression.

Depression is a desperate attempt by the emotions to force, through any means, hyperactivity or anger or both in forcing the release of pent-up competitive feelings.

Many competitive emotions are released on our expressways and streets, and maybe that's for the best, in some respects. Our society is rapidly losing areas where competitive emotions can be released. But in our rapidly changing American society we haven't come up with enough new situations to use up competitiveness, so even though it's rough driving on the highways with frustrated drivers, it's probably one of the few areas some of these people can still use for releasing these energies. We should very definitely find safer avenues for these people to get rid of these pent-up feelings, and since all men are naturally competitive, developing these areas is essential. To maintain a contented society these emotions must be released in man individually and collectively.

Some people feel the only way to release competitive energies is through sports. That is one way, but because of difficulty in getting everyone interested in sports and the fact that everyone is not always suited to sports we must find other ways. Really there are many ways in our daily lives at home or at work that a little adjustment could provide very suitable competitive release areas, and they don't have to be battlegrounds to accomplish this. Depending on a person's individual competitive needs, his particular ways of release must be determined wherever and according to his particular interests.

I've been working with people with developmental disabilities and mental illness in institutions and now in our own group home. I've always worked directly with people in helping them develop their daily living skills, schooling, day programs, and work skills. For over thirty years I've observed what motivated them and how some of these people either progressed or regressed. I've learned certain formulas that would lead to success if followed. These observations are strictly my own. I also want to explain that I'm not going to delve into all of our emotional releases as I see them, but primarily I want to basically stick with competitive emotions. Any other emotion will just be used to illustrate how I see the competitive emotions being displayed.

Also, I want to emphasize that this is not technical information that psychologists or psychiatrists or social workers use, but only information that came to my attention as I helped and observed people I worked with over the past thirty years. A quick explanation of how I view these areas:

All mental thought is dominated by the emotions. Emotions are expressed physically through learned behavior. All expression has emotional overtones. All expression has emotional competitive interaction entwined either in a noticeable way or at least in a latent potential, waiting to come into effect at the first opportunity.

It seems the emotions always dictate thoughts. First the emotions are activated by our senses. The senses that activate thoughts primarily are sight and hearing, and also others in different degrees. Then these impulses start going through the mind, picking up all relevant information that could possibly be similar and finally formulating in the brain a complete pattern. This area is the conscious area. So all thought originates in the back of the mind and moves forward through it, gathering information of a similar nature.

In all actions of a person, no matter what emotions are activated, competitive energies are present, but only to the degree that the situation demands.

All competitive emotions are released in the mind according to the need of each individual. If a person's lifestyle changes, the need for release could also change. If these energies are not expended, the building up of more frustrations takes place. When this happens, former release methods no longer suffice and more strenuous release alternatives must be introduced. If this is not realized in time, serious depressive moods can develop; then, if this is not realized, seriously detrimental escapism starts creeping in.

People don't like to change from one form of competitive release to another, especially when feeling depression or failure. I have noticed this particularly in men who need to change their attitudes toward job or marriage and reorganize their thinking in these areas. They become so desperate trying to hold onto their job or marriage the wrong way, and they're afraid to change their tactics, even though they're losing the whole battle. Generally they end up losing just like they thought they would, mostly because they became too afraid to change. Here is where a counselor must use great caution in giving advice.

Many of us would like to be boss or king of the hill; from childhood on, we have this urge. Many of us, as we grow or develop, have a tendency to develop certain methods and ways that enhance our competitive abilities to give us an advantage in life to achieve our goals and ambitions. This striving of our personality is natural, and everyone expects everyone else to act this way. When we achieve our goals, others give us recognition for having reached our goals, which took competitive energy to achieve. This striving is so natural, we don't even notice this competitiveness around us; we just think it's normal, and it is, and since it's so much a part of life, we don't notice it. So all our goals, our efforts, every purpose we have, need these competitive energies to exercise them in order to fulfill our daily existence. This is a normal reaction, to an extent, but when we allow ourselves to become too competitive, this feeling is detrimental because it destroys normal opposition and doesn't create an atmosphere for supporting others and normal relaxation of our own emotions.

People who have reached king-of-the-hill status no longer release competitive energies properly and so experience a great deal of struggle acting normal, not knowing why they feel so frustrated, having it made, so to speak. Unless they develop competitive release programs, they're in trouble.

No one, not even fairly young people, can handle this imbalance. I've seen fairly young people have to drastically change their lifestyle and go through very rough times, sometimes turning to serious escape devices, mostly alcohol or other drugs, to get relief.

Communist governments have problems in their societies because their constituents cannot find enough ways to release competitive energies. They have everything supplied, food, housing, jobs, etc., eliminating the striving that takes place in a capitalistic government. But when a capitalistic government becomes too monopolistic or monopolizes too much power, it also takes away the opportunity for the people to release competitive energies. When this happens, the same thing happens as in a communist government. People start getting frustrated, not knowing why. Even though these governments could be supplying all physical needs, still this is not what completely fulfills the emotional needs in man. Governments should not be suppressive but create avenues of opportunity to release competitiveness.

A lot of people in our inner-city areas are becoming more and more frustrated. They have no competitive goals. Or if they do have goals, these goals are so unrealistic that they are completely unobtainable. Since due to lack of schooling or training some people can't get a job, then frustration builds and urges to compete become stronger, so they end up quite often shooting or killing others by some means over card games, gambling, girlfriends, etc. This is all due to the fact that they don't know how, or can't, release competitive energies in an acceptable fashion. Unless the government realizes the desperate situation developing in larger and larger areas of our cities, the outcome can only be outbreaks of violence, possibly riots, or worse.

I wrote this book to see if there are others who are interested in what I'm saying and thinking. If so, I would like to get together with them and discuss these ideas. These thoughts are strictly mine and do not come from a book or others and so they are not technical in any sense of the word and are strictly observations indicating the way that I look at things. These ideas are based on my observations, having worked and observed people directly in their living units in institutions, day programs, and group homes.

The major differences between men and women's brains are caused by the emotions. The emotions seem to have more control over our lives than we think, even developing minor changes in the brain. The difference in emotions between men and women is major, but there are hardly any differences in behavioral learning areas of the male or female brain. Arriving at different conclusions and methods is due mainly to the emotions.

The mind works primarily by motivation of the emotions, through the senses, and forming ideas as it travels forward through the brain in the areas where awareness and formulating of ideas interact. So it seems that the emotions pretty much govern our thoughts and lives. Emotions work through learned behavior, and this decides why we do things in certain ways. I have only used the emotion of competitive energy in my examples in this book, but a lot of other emotions are probably more important. The reason I used basically the emotions of competitive release was their importance to our feelings of well-being, not because competitive energies are more important than any other emotion.

Another part of our emotions is our personality. Someday I would like to describe the overall personality and its relationship to the emotions. Personalities are as much a vehicle for the mind as competitive energies, or perhaps even more of a vehicle. All personality types come basically through our emotions, and it can be explained how the emotions are involved in them.

Personalities break down into three distinct categories. The distinctions are:

1. Type—the most important
2. Tendencies—the second most important
3. Character—the least important but the most recognized part of a personality

By being able to discern the difference between these features of the personality you can determine the reactions between people. Personality types react the same to other personality types; tendencies react toward other tendencies in the same manner, like or dislike, the same with the character. By knowing the reactions of these three distinct parts of the personalities it is possible to determine the type of relationship that will develop when people come into contact with others. When you are able to predict this outcome, it is possible to determine ahead of time one's competitive relationship with others.

I have brought personalities into this book because it seems to some people that conflict between personalities is one of the main reasons for mental problems. Instead, improperly developed learned behavior, during the formative years, seems to be the greater cause of emotional problems.

Mental difficulties seem to develop because of incompatibilities between learned behavior and our emotional feelings. Since emotional feelings are innate and can't be changed, we have to take into account the altering of our current learning process. Since early patterns of learned behavior can't be changed, we must also take that into account. We must deal with emotional feelings we generate, plus subconscious early learned behavior and our current learning, to make everything compatible enough so as to make us normally functional in a competitive manner.

Older people have many problems in changing their competitive releases when they retire. Unless they can come up with strong interests or hobbies, husbands and wives often start competing against each other and then one or the other starts holding or trying to restrain his or her emotions and this knocks him or her out of emotional balance. When this competitive balance is upset in older people, it leaves the door open for more imbalances and diseases of the mind, which normally wouldn't have much of an effect on them if they had been more active individually.

Competitive release can be seen in prizefighters: Before the fight, they seem to hate each other, glaring and acting hostile toward one another; they have developed a mutual hatred. After ten rounds of pounding on one another, when the fight is over, winner and loser kiss and hug each other. Why? Because of exuberance over the release of competitive energies. This is noticeable among all people who release competitive emotions against other individuals. First come the strong antagonistic feelings, then, afterward, often extremely friendly relationships. The same could be said for any people involved in strenuous, challenging competitive endeavors.

Schooling is considered a very important goal in the Western world, including the United States, and it should be. But it becomes almost the only goal for youngsters. Should *that* be? Since a lot of youngsters don't like school, there should be alternative areas of education where they can release competitive energies. Since there aren't alternatives in our society, youngsters build up inordinate amounts of frustration. When there is conflict, there should be interactions of some nature to regulate and release this competitiveness. When there is no release, frustration builds up to dangerous levels, and normal avenues that had been used to release competitive emotions no longer work for the youngsters. Then new avenues have to be explored. Our society should develop programs for dropouts from our competitive school system that can be useful to our society and fulfilling to the individual. Unless we develop competitive release programs for everyone, we will have a stressful, resentful group of young people who will turn to less desirable avenues to release these compulsive emotions.

Interesting reactions involving release of competitive

energies are seen in the relationship between a girl and a boy. A girl's main interest in a relationship with a boy is the release of her competitive energies. You say, "How?"? Well, let's investigate. First, a girl is not interested in just any boy; she wants a specific boy. She can describe him very well, and by emotional interaction she knows when she finds him. She may make a mistake selecting him by physical appearance, but after a short time of interacting verbally, her emotions will decide whether she likes him or not. This is the key: if he will satisfy her emotionally. She may give you some reasons for liking him that don't make sense. A lot of boys could fit a physical image, but what she wants is not really physical; it's emotional gratification. Most dissatisfied women, when asked why they're displeased with their husbands, are vague, but what comes through is that they believe their mates act like naughty children. Even when a husband, with whom a woman can release competitive emotions, becomes abusive, many times she really doesn't want to leave him, because he fulfills a very important need, as she has to release this energy. A woman will divorce what appears to others to be a decent, nice man and then remain with an abusive one to fulfill these emotional needs. Women will try to keep themselves pretty, trim, and charming in an effort to attract the right man, even at times using physical, sexual attractiveness in their efforts. The man the woman decides is right for her and is her type always fits her idea of a strong personality, her king-of-the-mountain type, whom she can use to release competitive energies. Men, instead, generally use their work areas or sports to expend large amounts of competitive energies. A person can use other sources also, but these sources must provide a resistant challenge if they are going to accomplish this need.

Even during normal conversation, competitive energies are present. If the conversation should turn argumentative and/or become more stressful, competitive emotions will be pumped up very quickly. That's why to remain emotionally healthy, a person must find challenges that will allow release of these competitive energies.

The best friends are those we have the best interaction with, not with one-sidedness but competitive interaction, generally over common interest and challenges. Being able to release competitive energies in friendly relationships is very rewarding. One-sided relationships do not release competitive energies. Most people see the release of competitive energies in sports only. This isn't so. Competitive energies or emotional feelings are released to some degree in all expression. The old saying "man is naturally competitive" is true, and he releases this energy in everything he does or says to some degree.

Competitive energies are released through learned expression, not innate knowledge. The rich and leisure class often show their emotions through good manners, etiquette, etc. The educated do it by what they learn through books, the poor generally through what they learn on the streets. So all emotions are shown through learned behavior. The difference between learned behavior and emotions is that emotions must be expressed; if not, they build up frustrations. Competitive emotions are dispersed throughout all expression, being intertwined with the rest of the emotions, and must be expressed or frustration will build up. This frustration will force a release of these competitive emotions, or if they are not released, then depression will set in, a desperate device of the mind to try to release these emotional needs.

All parents should pay attention to their youngsters and help them get involved in seeking to achieve whatever goals and challenges they can handle. If you observe your children enough, you'll see areas where they seem to try the hardest, relax the most, and get the most satisfaction. These areas are probably the best areas to encourage to help develop a relaxed child. Don't wait until youngsters start developing bad habits from peers in order to release competitive expression. It's true that areas of challenge to release competitive energies will be found, but these bad habits won't help the child or society, being negative, and they're much harder to get rid of before he can get involved in acceptable patterns that will accomplish the same competitive release for him.

The signs of competitive interaction begin early in life through innate behaviors: a toddler arguing with his or her mother, later playing mother against father, one sibling against another, playmates against playmates, etc. If you pay attention you'll see it constantly in the child's actions, but if you don't observe, you won't even notice such common actions because you will be so used to it.

Sometimes when a son or daughter is not getting enough competitive interaction with his or her parents or society, the child will display rebellious feelings in destructive or sexual actions. These are really desperate means to gain interaction with or positive attention from his or her parents or environment. Unless the child can gain this competitive interaction, he or she will become more depressed. Within every relationship there is interaction taking place unless, because of conflicting personality types, there's no interest in each other, and then negative feelings develop between people.

A father who considers himself the leader of the family is often confronted by his son. Sigmund Freud commented on hating your father. Often the reason that this develops— in many young men, not all—is the difficulties in the competitive interaction that takes place in a boy's mind in his early years. As his adolescent competitive emotions start developing, he begins competing for the attention of his mother. He actually competes for her attention, not quite understanding why he has this subconscious competitive emotion. Why he actually competes is not always recognized by his father or himself, and sometimes this competition actually develops into a small war. Tolerance of our feelings must be expressed through learned behavior.

The correlation between competitive release and mental health was evident when I increased competitive challenges to individuals with emotional problems. Others noticed it, too, and would relate that the individual with emotional problems didn't seem as disturbed as before and of course his or her attention span increased greatly, while emotional changes or mood swings were hardly noticeable.

Being put on the defensive occurs when you feel ill at ease with another and that you are being used emotionally. When you enjoy another, you act on the offense. You can tell rather quickly who you like and who you don't like by how you feel as you talk with them. The best is the give-and-take relationship, when you feel comfortable and the other person feels likewise. There no one is emotionally using the other. This mostly has to do with personality types when offensive and defensive competitive energies are being used equally. One of the most noticeable areas of reactionary defensive positioning is in marriage. When a woman uses sexuality too often, she may lose her enjoyment in the marriage by becoming frustrated due to being put on the defensive over sex. There is a rather easy solution by which she can fulfill her desire for a stronger relationship that offsets and defeats the sexual aggressiveness in men. The solution, of course, is to set up family goals where competitive energies can be released.

From a very early age children display emotional competitiveness. They will drag clothes off of furniture, throw toys, pull kitchen utensils out of cabinets, and argue with their mothers when getting their diapers changed. This is all the beginning of release of these competitive energies, through this disagreeing and arguing with the mother. As children grow older, they develop particular methods by which they release these energies according to their abilities and environment. Forming new patterns in their abilities and environments changes throughout life.

Remember, if your child feels down a little too often, you should take it seriously. What it might mean is that he or she isn't getting rid of enough competitive energies and that you must help him or her find acceptable avenues in order to release these energies. The consequences of failing to deal with this could be emotional problems. That is why we have so many teenage suicides and escapism in unacceptable behavior. When the latter happens, we have a tendency to restrict the young person. This is harmful, as he or she is already building up too much anger and frustration. This frustration buildup will force the child to find some release areas. Often you'll be given the advice, "Just let the child express him[her]self." This will not work unless the child just happens to find a hobby or friend who will help him or her find a competitive release that is acceptable to you. But this is chancy. Often what the child needs is support to get going in the right direction; otherwise, he or she will go astray and become afraid and fearful of thoughts that the frustrations bring to mind.

Competitive interaction between husband and wife often deteriorates, sometimes by the husband not performing his role. Though he often acts as provider, he must take an interest in the family not only in a financial way, but also in a positive interactive way. This provides a natural method of competitive release for the wife. If he is not providing this emotional release needed by the wife, he will automatically fall into the role, in her life, of one of her kids. She will not like this turn of events, even though she might have subconsciously encouraged it. But because of the lack of her husband's initiative in interacting on an adult level, he will automatically fall into another emotional level, that of a naughty child.

Learned behavior developed early in our lives can't be changed too easily, but we can analyze it and its detriments so as to add to this early learned behavior enough correct new information so that we can keep our emotions controlled somewhat according to the way we would like them to go. So the more you analyze this early learned behavior, the more you can determine what new information you can organize in your mind in order to present your emotional feelings in a more beneficial way. This new information must be learned thoroughly so that the mind uses it in conjunction with the negative early learned behavior and emotions that cannot be erased.

It used to be when a person had mental problems he or she would be put in an institution until he or she got better. Then the doctors found out that if they didn't release the person after a month or two they might as well forget him or her, because he or she would become chronic. Now the treatment is mostly day care, with the patient out in the public the rest of the time. The reason they had to do this was because plenty of rest and freedom of expression was not enough to achieve mental health, for only out in the public did a patient have a chance to get involved in competitive interaction and the release of these emotions. Expression is not enough; competitive avenues for relaxing this expression is needed. Interaction is needed or these emotions will build up and form a permanent block to the normal mental processes.

We all have built-in guidelines of emotional imagery that must be satisfied, as satisfying the emotions is necessary for inherited, innate imagery that is situated in each distinct emotional area. We have quite a few emotions, and most of the time they freely contribute their instigated compulsive needs to every thought that excites their particular pattern. The emotions won't be denied, they must be satisfied, and we must acknowledge this. But I'm not interested in these areas at this time. I'm only interested in showing the need for release of competitive energy, describing primarily this emotional need and its importance to mental health.

By undergoing the process of learning as much as you can about these releases and what triggers and motivates these emotions, then and only then can people explore how to change or create alternatives to the expending of these natural feelings. That they must be expended is obvious, but how they're expended is up to us, and the more we know the better we can set up their release in acceptable avenues.

I'm holding these illustrations short because I'm only presenting my views in a limited way and would then like to discuss with others who view these thoughts and ideas similarly to come up with a more positive presentation.

2

The Importance of Emotional Release

This chapter stems from my own personal thirty years' experience working with people with physical, mental, and emotional problems. I have had no "professional" training, although I have worked directly with physically and mentally disabled people. Because of my extensive experience, I believe I have something to offer to others who work in this field and to laypeople.

Early in my career, I observed what I believed were inadequacies in the way professional treatments were administered and the poor results obtained. The usual treatment consisted of rest and relaxation within a contained, secure, and comfortable environment, with plenty of supportive counseling. This treatment, I determined after a while, lacked one important ingredient. After several years of working and observing, I saw little improvement in the mental health of residents and outpatients. Their improvement was minimal. Outbursts of emotions and lack of confidence were still very evident, with no incentive to really improve themselves. By observation and experience I noticed that when people become involved in goals or interests, they show good progress. I also noticed an improvement in emotional behavior. I have concentrated on developing patient interest in setting and achieving goals.

Over the years I have seen that people with problems who succeeded were those who had set strong goals and strove to reach them. This also seemed to relieve emotional stresses. There seems to be a connection between competitive relief and the release of emotional tensions. The purpose of this chapter is to share observations so others may benefit.

I did not try to write this book in a scholarly way. Some people can talk about the common housefly in such a scholarly way you wouldn't know what they were talking about. My book was written very simply, trying to illustrate what I believe would strongly help our mental health situation.

Unless we change our current approach to mental health, we are doomed to failure. The number of mental patients is growing and we don't have enough prisons, and these are indicators of how we are dealing with mental disorders in our society.

Only through the strong motivating force of our competitive nature can we realize mental stability. This can not be accomplished through rest, relaxation, medication, or doing nothing but talking.

Some therapists start changing medications, hoping against hope to find something that might work. These are desperate attempts by therapists to find a means to mental health for their patients.

The natural laws are constant. Nature is not inconsistent. What applies to the body applies to the mind also. Healthful food and plenty of exercise means good development for the body and the mind also should be developed by learning and exercising its potentials. The muscles of the body when exercised properly will do what we want as we develop them. Our mind is similar: if we develop it with learning exercises, then all areas of the mind will work together to achieve success. The more we develop certain areas of the mind, the more we can expect from it, for it works primarily as a whole, just like the body. There are plenty of diseases and physical problems that happen to the mind, the same as the body, on a bad "diet." But not exercising the body and putting harmful food into it causes our body more problems than anything else. The same for the mind: the more immaterial matter we put in, the more trouble we will develop in our thought processes.

Our emotional input plus the different learning areas of the mind contribute to our thought process. The body develops muscles by using them, while our mind develops strengths through learning exercises. Our emotions contribute input to the thought process similar to the way our heart and other body organs contribute to physical performance of our muscles. We can accomplish no more than what the combined total of the emotions plus the learning areas of the mind will contribute. Some people develop bigger muscles and some bigger minds, but all of us can develop our minds and muscles somewhat and not doing so only encourages illnesses, physical and mental. In this chapter I'm only interested in how the emotions and mind contribute to competitive release, and that's why I bring in these illustrations showing rest is basically harmful to the mind unless it is used particularly well.

When you've formed an idea or thought, you will want to express that idea or thought. Also, you will probably be willing to defend that thought or idea. In defending a position, you solidify that position. Generally, if you are at all familiar with the subject you are discussing, you will defend your point of view quite strenuously. In arguing or defending your ideas against others, you're asserting your position and trying to make it more solid or defensive against attacks from others with different opinions. What I'm referring to is the amount of competitive interaction that is taking place. Even though subtly defending our ideas we don't look competitive, in talking about our ideas we offensively pursue and defend them. This is competitiveness even when accomplishing these actions very subtly. I believe that man is naturally competitive. The point I also want to bring out is that if a person doesn't like to argue or discuss ideas openly, what then? Or if he or she doesn't present his or her ideas very strongly, what then? Can such a person just sit on his or her ideas and feelings or does he or she have to find a way to release emotional competitive feelings. The answer, as you probably guessed, is yes, this person must find an avenue or interest to express or channel these strong inner feelings. Since the resisting and not releasing of these feelings or emotions through striving channels of expression can only lead to a buildup of anxieties or depressed feelings, then only through the use of competitive energies expended subtly or in more noticeable ways can we feel comfortable or normal. The buildup of these energies is unconscious, and if it is not used to express our feelings, we will develop frustrations and more serious complications in our mind, although we're not aware of it. So finding ways to express feelings is important, I feel, because not doing so can lead to explosive outbursts of emotions which will not be complimentary to oneself or others when finally expressed.

The differences between normal subtle expression of our emotions and full-blown expression of our emotions can be brought into play by something as trivial as the frustrating interjection of an insult or another irritating event suddenly happening. A shot of adrenaline courses through our bloodstream, and our subtle expression suddenly becomes highly competitive and explosive in nature and possibly very dangerous. So remember, when frustrations or emotions are built up the release of normal subtle expression can be altered drastically, and our subtle competitive expression suddenly becomes very highly competitive. This is normal, but we have to learn self-control when these shots of adrenaline hit our normal subtle competitive forms of expression. Especially if we are under stress of one kind or another and have a buildup of emotions, our expression could cause serious consequences in our relationships to others. Trying to find something competitively relaxing, striving after a goal, an interest where competitive energies can be gotten rid of before adversely affecting relationships with others is a healthy approach, in my opinion.

Due to a changing society, frustrations will build, and due to a lack of normal release, they will continue to grow. We must come up with new releases for frustrations, or they will vent themselves in many undesirable ways. For example, people will become more brusque or abrasive in their relationships with each other due to irritations and frustrations building up. These emotions build up due to a lack of normal release, which has been discarded with no substitutions being created to replace it. Even though going to sporting events and different gambling games provides for release of our competitive feelings, this generally happens too infrequently to provide enough emotional release. Release must be provided constantly in our everyday life.

Athletes who play professionally do release plenty of competitive energies, and that can be seen in their more relaxed attitude in talking to others. But our society as a whole must also have ways of venting its frustrations in everyday living, for in a changing society too many of the old ways that had been used to vent feelings in the past have been done away with. In the past, people were taught that being patriotic was important. Also, religious views were very strong and political arguments were important. People had serious views on these subjects and lots of other points of view on less crucial matters and would argue strongly over their points of view without disturbing anyone seriously. It was normal to do this. This relieved a lot of emotions. Now these differences are no longer considered, so we no longer defend these viewpoints and consequently don't release emotions. They build up with no way of releasing them.

Infighting and petty arguments are nonproductive ways of using competitive energies. Today we seem to have too much infighting with everyone we meet, due to a lack of larger goals. When people don't have large goals by which they can release competitive emotions, then they will start a lot of infighting over petty goals. These are generally arguments over minor, unimportant goals that appear when larger goals, requiring cooperation, are not practical. Where large goals involving many people are achievable, infighting is minimized drastically. If larger goals are constantly available, then people get out of the infighting habit. Most people don't like infighting as a way of releasing competitive energies but only do it because of the lack of major goals and a need to release their pent-up emotions.

An example of this might be the quick drawing together of people when a war breaks out. People band together in patriotic groups. They all strive together, releasing competitive energies.

Concerning the pupil-teacher relationship, what is the competitive interaction here? I believe that unless the teacher assists the pupil or student in achieving goals, the relationship will be poor. The better the instructor is at helping the student achieve learning goals, the better the relationship between the teacher and the pupil. Why? The student will feel good about releasing competitive energy in striving after these goals and because of gratitude, credit the teacher as an important part of this. Releasing competitive energies is the reason the pupil feels good. Rendering help in getting the pupil to do so is the goal of a good teacher, and this effort or striving is what makes the student release competitive energies. The harder they each strive, the better they feel. The less each strives, the worse one or both will feel, as no competitive energies are being used and a negative attitude will develop.

It is my opinion that all relationships are based on this release of efforts. So it is also obvious to me that with this mutual relationship, when both partners are releasing competitive energies, even love develops. If love develops in only one of the partners in a relationship, that means one person is using the other as a goal of pursuit and releasing competitive energies; only the one who strives will feel love. The other is not doing any striving so will not feel good about the relationship. To evaluate and help an unbalanced relationship, striving is needed in both people or in all parties concerned to get release. If a person cannot strive after the other person, neither will he or she feel love for that other person.

Even the collapse of communism occurred because there was not enough competitive release in the system. There is more competition in capitalism; communism has little competition. The people of communist Russia felt they had second best and didn't like that. Also, the communist government kept setting up five-year plans, and since communism is really noncompetitive, the people didn't try, as a whole, and the five-year plans never worked. The only competitive thing the communists had was a defense system.

You can understand why a bad person like Hitler succeeded. His many goals were what got the German people to support him. Even though they might not have liked all of his goals, they were attracted to some. Hitler's hidden goals they didn't know. He fooled the world, for a while. Since Hitler was a great manipulator of the emotions, he got many to release their emotional stresses by striving for certain goals. So it was in accordance with competitive emotional release that he was able to get people to support him. This is what commits people, this feeling of relief they get in striving to achieve. That is why it is important to be discerning, to be able to identify "real agendas" and not be fooled by stated goals, which often mask hidden goals, but goals attract people and we all have the tendencies to follow goals.

In our own society, with so many changes taking place, a lot of former competitive avenues have been discarded, and people are very mixed up, generally following others and/or looking for release in many diverse areas that aren't satisfying. Finding no release, they continue searching. We must search out better avenues for natural release or suffer the consequences.

Thoughts develop, I believe, to release our emotions and must do so. Our emotions demand that they be expressed; otherwise emotional turmoil develops in our minds in the forms of anxiety and/or depression. Since verbal expression is needed to relax our emotions and thought patterns are the means by which this happens, we should be careful about learned behavior. Thought patterns develop in our emotions basically through early learned behavior. We should be careful about the diet we give our children's brains when the emotions are first forming their expressive needs and dictates. For instance, suppose early in life you experienced a serious scare. This would enter into your emotions and affect you the rest of your life. Say you had a serious personality clash with your mother or father as you were growing up. This also entered thought patterns that dictated emotions later in life. Say later in life you marry a wife or husband who not only reminds you of past feelings, but seems worse. These problems, due to dictates from your emotions, plus your current dilemma, would be too much for you to handle. So you might do something drastic, just to release these feelings. What I am trying to do in this book is make it possible to live with problems by relieving emotions of added pressure. You can live with problems if you don't build up added emotional stress. My book won't solve your problems; it will only let you live with them so that you won't be forced into a bad situation. Lots of people who keep their emotions relaxed, through competitive releases, live with serious problems all their lives and are not forced to do anything by their emotions. Even if you do something for a deep-seated problem, it will be easier without extra emotional stresses.

I remember watching a little of the Jeffrey Dahmer trial on TV, and I won't try to summarize it, for it was extremely bad, but what he seemed to need the most was a friend or two whom he could interact, compete, and release his emotions with normally. But he couldn't because of a fear complex created early in his life, which he couldn't adjust to emotionally, so he was unable to make friends. He should have received help early in life for this. Anyway, I noticed the only victim Jeffrey intended to kill and didn't was the one he struggled and wrestled with. He was asked why he let this intended victim go and didn't kill him, and Jeffrey's answer was that he didn't feel like it. The real reason was that during his wrestling and striving with his victim he released enough competitive and pent-up emotions that he no longer felt compelled to kill. Since this only relieved his emotions temporarily, his emotions again built up and forced him to continue killing others.

I believe that thoughts are formulated by use of different opinions and experiences that we subconsciously feel will help us to obtain our objectives. Our thoughts are generated by an impulse of an idea, which goes through the mind picking up all relative feelings or impulses, as we formulate a conscious thought pattern. Since we use a lot of prior information we have experienced and developed over our past, we feel we can use them safely. If we are told by someone else to do something differently, we generally reject these suggestions until we have subconsciously run them through our prior experiences. If they trigger negative responses, only a great deal of new learned behavior can get us to use these new ways of doing something, because it must fit into a wide range of emotions and the rest of our mind, which uses this information competitively.

In my opinion, we are strongly influenced by our emotions as we think. Thought patterns formed in each emotional area are triggered when we rationalize or think. The impulses from our emotions are dictatorial, and we must accept them in our reasoning as we think. When these thought patterns are formulated in a disorganized way early in life, they will still influence our thinking all through life, so these early developments of our emotional thought patterns are extremely helpful or harmful to our whole life. Thought patterns are always established in accordance with our emotional needs. Our emotions will allow no thought patterns to form except along their own innate guidelines. Once the emotions have developed a thought pattern, it will enter our thought process in a subconscious way. We won't always understand why we feel a certain way and often make up excuses for our negative or positive thoughts, but it is really due to early learned behavior previously accepted into our emotions.

When we don't use our minds in a rational way, we can fantasize or daydream instead. Fantasizing doesn't use the whole mind, because we're not able to put these fantasy thoughts into performance physically and immediately, but only part of the mind. Since the whole mind is not being utilized when we fantasize this way, this information generally goes into the memory, and we may use it later, if we like it or not, depending on our will and emotions. The more we use this area of the mind, where we fantasize and more memories build up, the more the conscious part or reality area of our mind has a tendency to use this material. This fantasy material then becomes part of our normally stored thoughts due to the large amount of memory information we have developed due to the above normal use we have made of this fantasy area of the brain.

Since this information, which we have thought of over time, is immense because it was thought of so often, it could lead us to bringing into our rational thinking area of the brain thoughts that were fantasy and not reality-oriented and this in turn could confuse or make it impossible for us to use it in competitive action, thus making the person noneffective or mentally ill and not accepted normally. Sometimes these thought patterns are embedded in the mind. Unless we get better medications than we now employ, we won't achieve any kind of a breakthrough in changing these fantasy thought patterns in the brain once they are well established.

Patterns of thought are the way the brain likes to operate. The brain is set up to work best through developed patterns of thought or worked-out opinions helping it think. It does not like interruptions or interference when it is going through this chainlike process. In my opinion, when interference occurs, irritations and frustrations develop in the thinking process and will sometimes cause permanent damage to the thought process if no release is obtained. The release of these frustrations is through competitive channels the mind has developed from our earliest years, like sports interests or hobbies we participated in as children. If our current frustrations can't find a release, then the mind will not function or be able to rationalize properly. This was probably caused by interferences by either other people or events when the mind wasn't allowed to go through normal patterns of thought, so it will malfunction and become abnormal just because it was prevented from following normal patterns. There is a set, prescribed method the mind likes to follow when it develops a pattern. This is just plain, normal competitive thinking. When it is not allowed to function normally, due to interferences, the brain starts to form shorter, indecisive patterns that are not compatible with reality thinking, and this is detrimental to mental health, as once the mind is forced to form these new short patterns due to constant interference it can no longer go back to reality-based thinking patterns. When thinking patterns are developing in children with too much interference, it is extremely harmful to the child's mind. The child's mind is very different than the adult's mind, and so too much interference at these early ages can be very destructive because it does not follow according to their own awareness of reality. Ours, as adults, is much different and so we should not interfere or disrupt children's personal mind development. Interruptions by other children are beneficial because these interruptions are generally competitive in nature and, in my opinion, are healthy for them. Actually, too much help from adults is not beneficial, for it disrupts their young normal thinking patterns and takes them away from their reality orientation. Actually, people should not interfere in the lives of any loved ones too often, as this could disrupt thinking patterns and keep them away from reality orientation and normal thinking and keep competitive or goal-oriented thinking from being realized.

When you feel a person is drifting away from reality, in any manner, such as excessive daydreaming, try to get him or her competitive as soon as you can. Find pursuits and goals of interest, and this will help pull the person away from non-reality-based thinking patterns and into solid ones. Always give the person support in whatever he or she attempts to do, without being patronizing. Give real criticism and appreciation.

The mind is like the body. Just as the body does not use everything it eats, so the mind does not use everything it takes in, only material that fits into the emotional self-image of the person. Our mind or emotions select imagery that complies with what is being used in our own self-image or ego. Since some of our self-image and rationalizing is conscious, some is subconscious and controlled by our emotions, and this part and what it consists of we are not completely aware of. But it is evident that the emotions contribute a great deal to our rationalization and so we should find ways to keep our emotions relaxed or expressed so as not to build up unspent feelings that will further inhibit our thinking and degrade our self-image. Because as irritations and frustrations build up they have a tendency to make the ego or self-image a person has diminish. This in turn affects how a person interacts or competes with others.

Just going through the motions on a job does not mean you are releasing competitive emotions. If there is a lack of interest that you can't overcome, your job will only create more irritation in you and not release your emotions, for a job should be of a nature so you feel interest in it. But before you quit, try harder and strive to achieve. It may be you never really tried to see if you would like the job by working hard at it. If you are working hard and the irritations are occurring, causing disruptions, try to eliminate these disruptions carefully, as you can't express your emotions if irritations are stopping you from striving and showing effort on a job.

Rest and relaxation will not get rid of emotional stresses. My opinion is that only striving after goals will do the job.

During this age of affluence in our country, some people do not have to strive at making a living. Thus their emotions aren't vented through the competitive action required to survive in former times. Man throughout time has always had to strive to survive, struggling just to get enough to eat. In the past the average man didn't have the modern equipment and conveniences he now has, which lessen modern man's efforts to make a go of it. Welfare was also not available, making man strive harder to live. When certain changes took place, it lessened the amount of effort man needed to survive and also the amount of competitive effort needed to achieve a livelihood and excel. With the lessening of this competitive striving, there is a buildup of emotions due to less striving. We must find new avenues for these emotional energies to be released.

Not allowing a person to seek first minor goals and then harder goals or prolonging this process might lead that person into a chronic pattern of not being able to achieve anything. Delaying, prolonging, and resting are all very negative because often they lead to fear in our mind, for our emotions must justify our actions, or inactivity in turn enters our subconscious and creates more to overcome.

When you feel yourself being irritated emotionally by other people or something physical going wrong in your life to cause irritation and frustration in you and these emotions are ignored, eventually they will build up and cause depression. Am I then saying irritations, frustrations, and eventually depression are normal? Yes, in my opinion.

The reason the mind has these negative areas within it is to cause these feelings to create motivation in you. Irritation will motivate you, so will frustration, and if nothing else does, the dreadful feeling created by depression will force you to do something. If it doesn't, you had better seek help. These feelings are there to motivate you. Some of the great men of history were highly frustrated and even depressed at times, caused by their inability to find answers to their hard-sought endeavors, but because of the strong motivational forces of the mind, they were able to advance beyond normal achievements and find answers to impossible questions. But depression is serious. Address your depression and find goals for your life.

The amount of effort and striving zealously expended to achieve a goal is directly related to how much competitive energies are expended and relaxed feelings obtained. The more you put into it, the more you release emotional, competitive feelings and the more satisfaction you will derive. This in turn will show up in a positive emotional manner with others, because you will feel relaxed and be able to relate to others more normally.

When feelings of hostility or frustration are not released, they do not dissipate; they build up. When people try to hold in these irritated or dissatisfied feelings, these disquieted inner emotions become stronger. They won't go away by themselves. To rid the mind of these hostile feelings, challenges or strong goals are needed where competitive energies can be released, as these convey these hostile feelings out of the emotions and therefore the mind gets free of these pressures. Not doing so only lets these hostile emotions stay in the mind, and all the mind's energy is used to control or try to maintain a balance or rationalization of these emotions. When the person has to control his or her emotions because he or she hasn't expended them, he or she starts becoming physically less active due to using all his or her energies to control him/herself. Otherwise, the person just explodes, getting emotional or angry over minor incidents, unless he or she finds suitable goals to find release. The release of competitive emotions is therefore extremely important, because it conveys and carries all the other emotions along, as, in my opinion, the mind is naturally goal-oriented. The striving after these goals releases these emotions and gives a relaxed feeling to the brain.

If you feel you need to release your emotions because they're building up, because you lost your job or some other trauma has happened to you and you no longer have an avenue to compete in, be careful. Don't wait too long before you look for new avenues to release your emotions. The buildup of these emotions and frustrations will lead to forms of depression eventually. When this happens, it gets more difficult to release these emotions because of the abnormal buildup. Find a goal as soon as you can, but be careful not to take on any goal, for once a goal has been decided on it's hard to not continue, because you feel good releasing emotional energies. The good feeling is not because you're working on a worthwhile goal but because you're releasing competitive energies. This makes you feel comfortable and content.

Examine every goal constantly as you proceed to make sure you're not seeking to achieve a negative one. Be open, talk to others about your goals, try to take criticism without becoming discouraged, but the main thing is try to develop a goal on which you can expend a great deal of effort.

So remember, you will have a life of emotional problems if you do nothing after some trauma has happened to you. The best thing is to get your mind moving on goals. Forget your doubts, or at least put them aside, and get going on new goals and interests.

Man is often man's worst problem, because we try to help when we shouldn't. The problem lies in the way we channel or form thought patterns. We are so individualistic in how we think that any interference by others in how we reach conclusions is handled negatively by the mind. Even though we are a lot alike, we all think differently due to the different ways we form thought patterns, so the mind becomes irritated when we have to take too much direction in trying to accomplish our goals. Interfering in other people's decision making can be detrimental. Depriving people of their own thought patterns may cause irritation in their emotions. The best way to help people do something is just by making them do as much as possible themselves and limiting your support or help. If they can't do it, change the goal, but don't coddle them or be permissive. That would be very detrimental, as it would start failure thought patterns in the brain, which can only lead a person to hopelessness. A person must succeed in achievement of some goals, and our goal should be to help the person but not to do it for him or her, for the more the person does it alone, the more effort he or she uses and the better he or she feels. Too much direction only leads to disrupted thought patterns in the person we are trying to help, because this in turn does not allow his or her emotions to form the proper support for his or her own thoughts; therefore, he or she isn't able to rationalize normally.

Therapists should always in helping a person with emotional problems first start to determine that person's interests, then get the patient going and moving to develop these interests into goals. This starts releasing emotional pressure. By delaying this process with rest or inactivity, more emotional difficulties can occur, which could lead to a life of emotional turmoil, as these abnormal patterns become set in the brain. Putting a person in a mental hospital tends to be negative, as therapists there let people drag along in therapy so long that bad emotional patterns often develop and can become permanent. Therapists should help patients focus on stronger goals as rapidly as they can and get them away from their past failures and on to successful achievement of new interests and goals. So many therapists just seem to be bleeding the patient dry with no noticeable improvement, just taking the patient's money. Therapists mostly listen to the patient talk and give suggestions. This makes the patient feel better, but in a very temporary way, and in the long run it can only lead the patient on a never-ending road to emotional imbalances. It's almost as bad as putting him or her in a hospital; he or she will eventually become chronic. If therapists assisted the patient in setting stronger, realistic goals, the patient would experience stronger emotions and feelings again.

For instance, in a game of chess, if enough interest and striving are exerted in trying to win the game, a person could release more competitive energies than in a larger exercise with a lot of physical activity, such as golf or basketball. The release of these energies is in the effort and striving of the emotions. This striving relaxes the emotions, taking away emotional stresses.

Obviously, a person suffering from depression needs

to find more strenuous ways to compete than a person with fewer problems. Always remember, competing can occur in any process in life, but arguing or fighting is a negative way and does not provide enough release of pent-up emotions. Determining interests and abilities and planning toward developing these interests can be satisfying aids in getting rid of frustrations and depressed feelings. Then others will feel more comfortable and will relate to you in a more relaxed manner, as they will not feel your nervousness.

Emotional needs are dictatorial; emotions subconsciously convey imagery to the conscious mind. This imagery is dictatorial and must be obeyed. Most of the time we're not even aware of this information consciously.

We never question the feelings or impulses we get through our subconscious; we just incorporate them into our rational thinking. As each of our personalities is different, we select and store our thoughts differently. Information we take in is first interpreted emotionally in terms of the material we already have and then stored accordingly. When we use this stored interpreted material, it comes into our rational thinking area as it was interpreted and stored. Though we sometimes wonder how or why we feel as we do, we generally accept it "as is" and use it in our competitive endeavors, not fully understanding why, just thinking it must be right, but it's only according to our own emotions and from prior learned behavior. Since our emotions dictate how we feel and put this information into our conscious mind as we rationalize, we are somewhat surprised when we realize, all of a sudden, thoughts we didn't know we had arrived at, or how. So large amounts of learned behavior are accepted by our self-will and sorted out, stored, and eventually used by our emotions to contribute to rationalization. So our emotions do have a lot to do with our thinking process, as they add or subtract to our rationalization according to the information they have accumulated. And since this information may have originated early in life, we cannot seem to understand all of it, but our emotions will use it throughout the rest of our life, affecting our thinking.

Our government and politicians like to make promises and make things easier for us, but this will not encourage solid goals, which our society can strive after effectively and thereby release emotions. The same applies to the family: Not providing solid goals to work for and achieve and instead making things easier will not help your children relieve their emotions properly. When you do make things easier or more convenient for your family, at the same time give them new avenues and goals to strive after so you won't take away their means of keeping their emotions relaxed.

The relationship between man and woman can be highly competitive, in my opinion. Many women dress nicely and try to keep their figures more than men do. Why? Women work a lot harder on their looks and jealously look at other women to see how they're dressed. Why? The reason is so that other women won't best them with their dress and get more attention from men. Even when other women are dressing somewhat immodestly, some conservative women may follow suit because their unconscious competitive feelings get them to dress similar so as not to be outdone by other women in attracting men. Women are especially concerned that the man of their interest will not be attracted to another woman. Men are confused by this maneuvering and manipulation between women, not understanding why women dress and act the way they do, and think that women are acting sexier, which is upsetting and very disquieting to women. This is the main cause of frustration and even depression in many women, because they feel man is overly reacting to more modern dress styles among women than he should be. Men, on the other hand, are stimulated by sight and the more of the female figure they see, the more stimulation they feel. So you can see some of this modern style of dress should change to relieve the pressure on women and men both, but mostly it's taking advantage of women because they become the goal, wrongly pursued sexually by men because of this extravagant dress code, and this added defensive resistance starts becoming frustrating and depressing, with a feeling of no way out. That's why we have such a higher number of depressed women than men, this undue emphasis on sexuality, which creates a defensive feeling in most women.

Women compete with each other for men's attention, but they can only find out through personally talking and interacting with a man if he is the man they want. For just any man will not do, as many women who argue with themselves and others and marry the wrong man anyway find out to their sorrow later. Some men will pursue women for their looks. Some women will resist these advances because they have natural feelings about sex, their own figure, and looks quite different than men's feelings. These differences are necessary, for they create in man a desire to pursue a woman harder. This striving on man's part and natural resistance on woman's part makes a man use up competitive energies, making him feel good. Women, on their part, use this desire in men to get the right man to pursue them, as the sexual desire is much different in women and so they can actually manipulate these qualities of theirs to attract men, almost using them as a tool, somewhat as flowers attract bees. Since not any man will do, woman tries to dissuade men she doesn't want from pursuing her, and since her natural desire is to release competitive energies, she must pick a man she feels is naturally strong, personalitywise, and kind, so she can emotionally interact with him. This striving against his strengths gives her the feelings of relaxation she is after and will create in her feelings of love. But unless he has these emotional strengths she is looking for, she won't want him. Even if he had all kinds of muscles but not emotional strength, she would reject him.

It seems when two people marry, after a short time they often take opposing views. Generally one takes a more conservative view, sometimes the opposite of the other's. This seems to be helpful in solving goals. Without goals, a rewarding marriage is impossible, as the partners become entangled in petty arguments. Businesses are the same. Most of the time the boss is more conservative than his or her employees. This is also noticed in government. People take conservative or liberal views. They form this arrangement, it seems, because of problem solving. The positioning, it seems, leads to a better understanding of how to achieve goals. Goals are part of man's existence. Without striving, there is no release of competitive energies or good mental health, as this emotion is tied into the releasing of all the emotions. The building up of the emotions causes frustration and stress, leading to mental difficulties, including depression. Also remember, as our life changes, more irritations and frustrations could enter in, so we might need different competitive avenues in which to release all these added emotions.

Everything you form as an idea or opinion in your mind you set yourself up to defend or argue when talking to others. Why do we defend ourselves? Why are we so competitive? I believe the mind uses this competitive method to achieve goals and to release frustrations or emotions. Without the release of emotions, other, more serious consequences start developing. The mind uses no other method to relax itself. Either you release these different emotions or they build up in your mind. Holding them in can result in explosive actions, as they will only build up to a certain level. Holding emotions in means you have to use more and more control. This becomes very difficult and more effort will be needed as you try to hang in there. After a while the mind will develop devious methods just to release these emotional buildups, such as alcohol, other drugs, and other means of escapism. Finding acceptable competitive avenues and/or having goals or interests can be an aid to releasing frustrations. Suppressing emotions can lead to trouble. Letting them through acceptable channels, rather than outbursts of hostility, is healthier.

I've heard that 20 percent of the murders committed in this country occur during family arguments. Many times people murder someone they know well, and often love. What causes these serious consequences? The causes are disagreements that often build up over a period of time and then climax in anger and fighting. These disagreements are based on personal opinions that started with a minor opposing thought and slowly became more and more defensive as competitive differences grew. Pressures started to build. If other objective goals had been available to relieve these competitive energies and keep them from building up, serious consequences could have been averted. When people don't have common goals to vent their frustration on, then infighting and petty differences are used by the emotions to release these emotional energies. Common family goals are a better way to release competitive feelings than individual infighting. Unless common goals are provided that are acceptable to members of the family, people will start providing their own, which might be very selfish. When infighting is conducted in back alleys among gangs we are appalled, but our society is starting to develop infighting even between different sections of our governmental departments. The public is viewing the government's infighting seriously, as it does not achieve common goals. They feel a lack of confidence, therefore breeding more public unrest and distrust.

Suicides and murders are becoming more prevalent. Most people who committed suicide felt there was nothing for them in life, no hope, as they failed at everything they tried to do. Others around them, family and friends, often offer moral support. But the suicide victim feels no one understands. Life is purposeless. The real reason the person feels this way is because he or she has no interest or goals to strive and put forth effort to achieve. Without this, he or she builds up emotional frustrations, which kills him or her inside, causing depression. Man is made to strive. Teenage suicide, as well as murder, is getting out of hand. Society has no excuse for it; it is to blame for not providing worthwhile goals. Easy living and no goals will not provide the release of competitive emotions to relieve tensions.

I have also seen retired people who had a good education and skills and a profession and later in life went into a nursing home where everything was done for them and senility occurred, because of their lack of interests. Reminiscing, thinking about their past life, is detrimental. Getting interested in goals and personal interactions is necessary for personal health, no matter how old a person is.

Youngsters benefit from competitive pursuits. Striving for goals requires them to release their energies and/or emotions. If you can get your child interested in pursuing education, you will find he or she will use up his or her energies in some educational field, but one-half of our youngsters can't seem to use education competitively to strive after. This is too large a number to just leave to their own devices to come up with alternative competitive pursuits, and they must find a competitive pursuit if they want to stay emotionally healthy. That's why so many youth gangs take over, because the members release competitive energies against each other and other gangs. During these modern times of change we are also losing former methods where the public was involved emotionally and not replacing these areas where people could seek acceptable goals and keep emotionally relaxed. Previously, national origins were strongly defended, and strong arguments between husbands and wives did not supply a reason for divorce. I don't advocate going back to this, but our society, due to change, has done away with these ways while not supplying new avenues to release our emotions.

We should find new goals for our society to pursue, as this will relax everyone. Too many people in our society are feeling uptight and/or tense, and that isn't good.

When a youngster becomes a teenager, his or her body changes due to hormones; this also affects the amount of stimulant given to his or her expression. This increased stimulant changes the teenager's normal expression, which had been more subtle, to a more aggressive, competitive manner. We sometimes say the teenager is being rebellious; this is true in that his or her normal, subtle, competitive expression has now, due to stimulation, become more competitively aggressive. The only real change was the added stimulant, nothing more.

Are people competitive from day one of life? If so, it is natural. It's the main and only method used to convey feelings and thoughts. So it can be subtly seen in a child's personality from birth and is always present when he or she expresses his or her emotions. Only when he or she suppresses his emotions by doing nothing does he or she keep the competitive emotions in.

I worked for years with adolescents in institutions. Sometimes when I received a new resident at the institution he didn't want to come out of his room to participate in the programs, and I had noticed that until I got a new resident involved in interacting with others in the group, he wouldn't get better. So I would have to by different means, using others in the group or other methods, entice him out of his room, for as long as he remained in his room he seemed to get mentally sicker or just start going into more daydreaming or fantasy. Improvement only came from interaction through striving within the group and in planned activities. The more I could get him interested in others or some activity, the better he seemed to me and others working at the institution. The mind does not seem to be able to function properly when a person just sits idly around or has a very limited amount of self-expression. He or she will have explosive outbursts and then seem to go into escapism and fantasies. Therapists should strive to determine the talents and interests and gifts of mentally ill people and prescribe treatment that involves them in striving after and achieving goals the therapist feels they are capable of achieving. If the patient refuses, he or she should be told to seek the advice of another therapist and be discharged. Some therapists just milk patients for all the money they can get from them or their insurance company and will use the excuse that they really feel rest and quiet are the answer, at times just giving themselves an excuse to continue to charge a patient for long periods of verbal therapy, sometimes for years, without achieving any noticeable improvement in the patient. If people have strong goals and purpose, rest and relaxation are helpful, but if the person has weak or no goals, then rest and relaxation are very detrimental.

Even though we're not aware of it, in my opinion there is always a subtle flow of competition and manipulation between people when they're interacting with each other. We're unconscious of this subtle flow of competition, but if you observe carefully you can see it in the actions of people. Sometimes it is more obvious, whereas at other times it is hardly noticeable, but it *is* there.

Until man can feel comfortable by expressing his emotions, he will feel nervous constantly. This nervousness will make him feel like he should be on the move, doing something, anything, not knowing that his emotions are not relaxed and that this is causing his feeling of wanting to be on the go, always moving.

Just because you know that a depressed person needs

to get going on goals and challenges doesn't mean that the person knows this. He or she is confused. You must sometimes use all the knowledge you have to get the person started and to continue with your help until he or she gets going on his or her own.

Whenever you feel nervous or irritated with another person, try to think of some goal or activity that you can do together with that person instead of arguing or not talking to him or her.

To put the clamps on young people in ghettos is not a good solution, for you might stop some of the stealing and other crime for a while, but it will soon come back in worse ways, as you cannot suppress the release of competitive emotions for very long. Suppressing emotions is dangerous, because then they build up to explosive levels. Finding avenues of acceptable competitive release is a solution, in my opinion. Even if you could get enough police to stop young criminals, they would flip out and find irrational ways to vent their frustration through escapism, such as drugs or vandalism. There are no answers unless you replace the negative way in which they release competitive energies now and give these ghetto youths acceptable avenues such as programs like the Peace Corps or environmental conservation camps.

Our country is highly engrossed in solving mental health difficulties. The beginning of this endeavor worldwide was with Sigmund Freud, who died in 1939. He was the Austrian neurologist and founder of psychoanalysis who first started trying to diagnose this dilemma. Intellectuals in this country got interested and began many different treatments in this relatively new science. Poor mental health is caused by the concept created by our mental health professionals of this country who feel that by resting the mind and giving people with mental difficulties relaxation, they can heal the mind, when in fact the mind is similar to the rest of our body. If we let our body go, it will become fat and weak. The mind is similar; if we only rest and relax our mind, it will become frustrated and disorganized. Our minds need goals and interests and encouragement to stay healthy. Rest and relaxation are the worst methods possible. We need nationwide goals to unite us and strong motivation from our social health people to heal our society.

So I end this chapter by saying that plenty of rest and relaxation, not putting pressure on the person, and giving him or her plenty of supportive counseling will not work in our mental institutions, correctional facilities, or public schools. This will not work because the therapists have forgotten that man must compete and strive to relax his emotions. Rest and relaxation are fine only when competition and striving after strong goals relax your emotions first.

3

How Does the Release of Competitive Energies Relate to Mental Health?

Is there a connection between the releasing of competitive energies and mental health? We know that man is naturally competitive. How ingrained in his intellect is this need? Is his need so great that unless he can release competitive energies he won't achieve decent mental health? If he doesn't compete enough, does this mean his mind will not function correctly? Will his mind start malfunctioning if he doesn't use his natural competitive energies as he should? How can he determine if he is using up his competitive energies or if they're starting to build up in his emotions? Can he sleep and rest a lot without it causing mental difficulties? Should he spend time listing goals, pursuits, and objectives he's interested in and would like to accomplish? If he feels too emotional, does this mean he should look for stronger goals to pursue? Does that mean strong goals are needed to relax traumatic emotional events that happen to him? If traumatic things happen to him and he feels like brooding, sleeping, or resting, could this be emotionally harmful? How soon after crises happen must he start planning new goals or objectives to fill his time again? Isn't there any time a serious or traumatic event might happen when he can just sit and rest for a while? Why does he have to keep going? Can't he ignore nature or his competitive nature? When he sees others with emotional problems, should he leave them alone or help support them in their achieving goals? When helping another achieve a goal, should he determine the goal for the person or get him or her to set his or her own goal?

Since prevention is the best medicine, we should be extremely careful with our support of and interaction with young children. Thought patterns are formed early, basically as development occurs in a particular emotional need area. These thought patterns develop in the emotions as a youngster moves from one growth stage to another. You might notice how cautious, reserved, or hesitant a child is very early in life. Reserve, hesitancy, bashfulness, or holding back indicates when a child is developing emotional thought patterns relating to his or her feelings of security. It may seem on the surface the child is just being careful before developing his or her relationship with you further, but he or she really is forming thought patterns, learning how to develop trust or fear and how he or she will interact personally with others throughout life. If this period of early life is traumatic, due to abuse or other unsettling problems, this will enter the child's subconscious, negatively affecting his or her security area of the brain permanently. Also, because this is an early stage of development for these security emotions, these early thought patterns will haunt the person the rest of his or her life if they're negative. If these patterns are normal and the child experiences a satisfactory stage of development during this period, he or she will more easily face traumatic events as they occur. Since development stages are gone through as a person grows, each stage must be handled differently, with the necessary support and encouragement. Not giving the proper support as a child goes through these stages will have a negative affect on his or her life, because his or her emotions will not respond positively to situations he or she is going through. I'm saying all this because it will affect his or her competitive striving after objectives or goals for the rest of his or her life. The most serious debilitating problems of the mind are formed early during the period when fear and security development of our emotions are formed into basic thought patterns. All these thought patterns formed in our emotions will influence our thoughts throughout our life through our subconscious. Since fear is so debilitating, it hinders us strongly from competing or going after our objectives normally. Other irritants and hindrances compound and keep us from accomplishing competitive endeavors and will be handled negatively by our competitive mind. If a person is subconsciously limited in his or her competitive endeavors, then everyday ordinary irritations will affect him or her more, and the chance of failing to achieve goals will be greater. Since failures bring in depression, careful consideration should be given to a child as he or she goes through each emotional development stage. As later stages of development are completed, it becomes very difficult to work around a damaged emotional thought area of the brain as the damage becomes permanent. Supporting these crucial developmental stages of the emotions is necessary for a good life. I don't understand why our emotional mind develops more thought patterns during certain periods as we grow, but it does, and these thought patterns control us the rest of our lives in a positive or negative way. So security and support, especially during these crucial stages, is essential to establish good mental health for your child for the rest of his or her life.

Man is goal-oriented and strives to succeed; thoughts of failure are rejected as weaknesses in his subconscious. When he does fail because of circumstances such as background, environment, education, or training, he may develop guilt feelings. These guilt feelings due to failing to succeed in achieving a goal are motivators of the mind, but since they're so irritating some people refuse to try again because they hate these terrible, depressing feelings. In fact, they are the biggest reason people won't try anymore. Since guilt feelings are so depressing, people who experience a high rate of failure often quit trying. Since man is goal-oriented and emotional expression is geared to striving after goals, not choosing goals to go after is really mental suicide. So people who live in a negative environment and can't find goals to strive after generally turn to crime or just sit around doing nothing. The challenging life of crime—dealing in drugs, gambling, stealing, evading the law and police—relieves more emotions than some low-paying, nonchallenging jobs. I've argued many hours with delinquents over this subject of stealing and came to the same terrible conclusion. They may not have had the chance to strive for jobs due to the negative environment and/or upbringing that Welfare forces on people. Welfare does not encourage people to try but penalizes them if they do by taking away their Welfare money. Welfare money should be used to continue help until the recipient is well established in new job pursuits of a challenging nature and will not feel he or she will lose out if he or she gets a low-paying job to begin with. Destroying man's incentive motivations is the same as destroying his life.

To maintain good mental health it is essential to express our emotions. This means we must learn how to release emotional feelings normally. Since man is naturally competitive, we must use these competitive urges as a means of releasing our emotions. Since man is naturally competitive, even when it doesn't seem evident in everyday living he is nonetheless using this system to release his emotions. Most of the time the flow of competitive emotions is so subtle we don't see or recognize them as competitive, but if you evaluate a person's actions carefully, you can see it more distinctly. As you notice this flow of competitiveness, you start realizing how important it is to man's emotional well-being to make sure this flow of subtle and more obvious, stronger competitive energies is not impeded but encouraged in normal everyday lifestyles. Planning goals for oneself and sometimes helping others find goals for their lives are essential for emotional well-being, for these are the only ways we can keep the mind from building up emotions, using this natural process of releases through competitive interaction. Sitting around will only build up emotional stresses, not relax them. The more anxious or depressed feelings we have, the stronger the need for stronger goals in order to express ourselves. Striving after difficult goals, not simple goals, is needed to relax and release these stronger energies of our emotions. I know at times when we're working with a person with troubles we want to tell him or her to relax and rest. But this is wrong and will hurt him or her in the long run. If we do give that person rest, it can only be for a day or two; then supportive goals must be encouraged. Tranquilizers can be prescribed, but mostly to carry the patient through the most difficult time as he or she starts to formulate goals. Goals, as soon as possible, should be strengthened to a more striving nature for better emotional results. As the patient becomes more relaxed, you can slow him or her down from striving after strong goals, but not until the patient's emotions show a decrease in anxiety. Start a person on supportive goals as soon as possible; otherwise his or her emotions could be affected; plus the patient will emotionally show signs of weakness by not wanting to compete as he or she once did. This indication of not wanting to get involved competitively in society is a sign that the patient was not helped soon enough after an emotional upset. If a patient, after help, does get involved in competitive goals on his or her own, he or she has recovered, will not seem emotionally weak to others, and will feel confident again. This is the best sign of mental stability.

What is it that causes us to fail when striving after goals? Failure to achieve one's goals seems the main cause of emotional turmoil. The biggest and most harmful cause seems to be irritations from other people. This irritation can occur in many forms, but when the irritation seems severe enough to make the other person quit attempting to reach his or her goal, that is the worst. Sometimes people don't like to say who or what caused them to fail and have emotional problems because of personal feelings, and really it's not that important anyway. The important thing is to start them or motivate them to start again. There are many irritating things capable of stopping or hindering us, but not many things will get us going again. Support the most important things; motivate and stimulate the person as soon as possible. For man is so competitive he's not always aware that he's hurt another person emotionally and stopped him or her from pursuing his or her goal. Sometimes he is aware of it, but it doesn't seem as serious to him as it should. If you see that you have hindered another person so as to stop him or her from continuing toward his or her goal, apologize and help support him or her to start again. This helping him or her will also make you feel good, as we are all social creatures.

Everyone releases competitive energies differently, according to their own particular emotional needs and abilities. Men seem to look for more physical releases than women. Women look for more social-minded ways to release energies. But in all emotional release there is a striving, an attempting to achieve or conquer or attain some objective. This is natural, for without this striving there is very little release of the emotions or other energies building up in the mind. The buildup of emotions and energies occurs when they're not being used properly. This can happen when we have little to do or if we have a nonchallenging job. If you have an easy job or no job and you are not striving after other goals, you can expect a buildup of tensions. This is nothing more than too much energy accumulating, which in turn triggers our emotions to build up and possibly explode. Some strenuous exercise, like body building or weight lifting, can be used by confined persons to find relaxation. For this is a way they can strive hard enough in confinement to find relaxation and relieve emotional pressure. For in the striving after goals, which is natural, we find emotional well-being, for man strives harder to achieve goals than any other form of life. Therefore, we can compete and win over all of nature, sometimes to our disadvantage if we're not careful. But it's only because of our strong competitive nature that we are able to do this. If we don't use this competitive nature, we won't use our brain normally and it will deteriorate, malfunction, and become useless to us. The less we use our competitive nature, the more emotionally depressed we will become. So therapists must determine what a depressed person's abilities and talents are and immediately start him or her going after goals. Prolonging therapies through rest and relaxation and the overuse of tranquilizers do nothing more than make the mind permanently dysfunctional. Once the mind is in this state of disability, we have no drugs or electric shock treatment that will rehabilitate it back to normal. Even though therapists estimate they help two out of three patients improve, this does not mean they help the patients completely back to their original mental health. This rate must be highly increased so that everyone who sees a therapist is helped, much more than this low estimate. Preventive therapy, keeping the emotions relaxed, is better than waiting for emotional turmoil and mental disabilities to develop. Prevention of mental illness is better than trying to cure it after it occurs.

Almost half the marriages in this country end in divorce, and many of these divorces are due to the spouses not being able to handle personality conflicts that arise. A lot of people who have divorced use petty arguments to explain why their marriage failed, but if you look closely, you will see that the differences between conflicting personalities are the main hidden cause. Some wives or husbands complain about all kinds of minor irritations they don't like about the other partner, plus more serious conflicts sometimes. But even working out these differences doesn't guarantee agreement. Some spouses just won't adjust to their partner's personality type. Personality adjustments would help more marriages than any other type of counseling.

Personality interaction begins deeper in our subconscious mind than is obvious, and to explain this phenomenon one has to understand what it entails and why we interact as we do. First, is it detrimental or harmful, this personality interaction? Yes and no. When another person interacts with you and irritates you a great deal and you try to stop that person with a bad attitude and he or she continues explaining that he or she likes you and is trying to please you and not trying to irritate you, how do you handle this? First of all, you can see the person is trying to please you. Why, then, do you feel so depressed and irritated at times over this interaction? Since this is a natural phenomenon between all people, personality interaction, how can you handle this confrontation, especially if it's severe and depressing you? And why is it taking place? A book could be written about personality confrontation, but simply, it occurs because someone is personally using you as a conquest or pursuit and being normally competitive and you resist. In attempting to please you and interact with you this person is actually, in an emotional way, confronting and pursuing your personality as a conquest goal. This confrontation subconsciously is taken negatively by your personality, because of our natural competitive instinct to resist such efforts, so you naturally become defensive against this person. Since you can't change your feelings, how do you handle this irritating emotional conflict you feel? You can't change your personality type or the other person's as you will eventually realize. And since these feelings will continue to build in your mind if you don't handle it properly, as your personality type will never change, what do you do? Basically, or to simplify, there are two ways to handle this conflict, and since the person pursuing you won't consider it a conflict, as he or she is enjoying this pursuit, he or she might not understand why you need to do something to change things. As this person enjoys pursuing you and doesn't understand why you get so defensive over it, maybe you don't know yourself and feel defensive or even guilty. So the first way you can handle this conflict and get rid of defensive feelings is by agreeing on a common goal that both of you can work at pursuing. Thus you can get this person's attention off you and relieve the emotional conflict you feel.

The second way that would help this conflict would be by trying to develop more separate goals so there will be less contact between you. Having plenty of separate goals will take the pressure off you. The best way to handle this conflict should be worked out mutually; otherwise it might generate more problems if you don't convince the other person of your emotional need. He or she might feel rejected personally and cause more conflict, which would be harder to handle and always detrimental and defeating for both of you, in the long run. Since this is a quick answer, much more time could be needed to explore emotional needs and goals of each person involved to satisfy individual cases than explained here. A book could be written about the many different personality conflicts between people and how to work out these personality differences. But once this is accomplished, what nice relationships can be forged by working out confrontations to a mutual understanding!

Lately there has been a fatalistic inclination or approach to mental illness, with the belief that one is born with a proclivity toward mental disease. This kind of attitude says there is nothing you can do about it, so you might as well accept it. We are all born with weaknesses, physical and mental, that can be overcome or strengthened. We are also born with certain abilities and strengths, and developing these will lessen the need to dwell on our weaknesses.

It can't be stated enough how influential our formative years are to good emotional health. It is during these years we learn to put together thought patterns that will influence how we will reach conclusions for the rest of our lives. It is also during this time that our emotions are being stabilized, which will influence our decision making for the rest of our lives. These emotional thought patterns developed early and will be used throughout our lives, helping us reach conclusions. The only way they can be modified or influenced is through positive recent learned behavior in the same emotional direction, since emotions can't be changed but only modified somewhat, based on careful understanding of what that early emotional behavior was. It is necessary to thoroughly understand early behavior so you can encourage the proper learned behavior that will help compensate for early emotional limitations. Without understanding early learned behavior, you won't understand why you're coming to certain conclusions and acting the way you are.

The emotions that seem to influence us later in life the most detrimentally are our feelings of security and fear, which were acquired early in life. Our emotions dealing with fear in our early life seem to be the most damaging to our emotional actions in later life. When a child is young, insecurity seems to be one of the most prevalent feelings.

This is understandable, because children are always getting hurt or scared, due to the fact that they can't protect themselves and really aren't capable of understanding enough to know how to prevent themselves from getting hurt or into trouble. Childhood also is a time when it is so easy to develop fear patterns that will influence the person for the rest of his or her life. Mostly we don't remember or know when we first developed these early emotional patterns, so sometimes it's puzzling, later in life, to understand how we got them. As we mature and grow, in life we might run into more circumstances that might reinforce these early fears imprinted in our minds. So by the time we're adults we probably have in our emotional thought patterns some potently limiting areas that will restrict our lives because we feel insecure about what happened as we matured. We now feel this insecurity, mostly subconsciously, and compensate by overdevelopment of a system of defenses and strengths to resist these weaknesses we developed emotionally, not realizing we subconsciously did this to compensate for the insecure way we felt. So most of our emotional strengths have developed due to inadequacies or weaknesses that we have overcome and learned to live with. This is normal and it does help us to overcome where we feel weak emotionally, due to some early unfavorable experiences. But a lot of fearful, bad events that happened to us early in life we never will be fully aware of. So these early fear-creating impressions in our feelings will create insecurity and inadvertently influence us for the rest of our lives, in a subconscious way, affecting unfavorably how we think and reach conclusions. If we become aware of these negative emotions and learn new methods that will help handle these negative feelings so they don't control as much, then our competitive goals will be easier to achieve and these early fears won't hinder us in achieving our pursuits and goals. If you know that you had abusive or fearful things happen early in your life, you should realize your emotions have been influenced. Realize also that later in life these fearful abuses will hinder and irritate or prevent you from achieving your goals. Try to prepare yourself by developing long-range goals involving other people, allowing other people to help you by keeping you on your goals and helping you overcome your weaknesses as they come out. This will also help keep these abuses from stopping you and causing emotional buildups throughout your life.

Abusing a child creates a lifelong deterrent to emotional security. Frustrated, angry people are the cause of most cases of abuse. Emotional energies that aren't released normally will build up and come out through bursts of frustration and anger, sometimes toward innocent people. The best way of controlling these frustrations is to get rid of energy buildups. Expressing oneself in a natural way will get rid of these emotions. Expression is best released through striving to achieve goals. This exercises the emotions the best. A society is made up of individuals, but a society's failure to provide solid goals for growth and social expression will always display itself in excessive violence and individual outbursts. In a society, as striving goals disappear, due to affluence and prosperity, one can look for violence and abuse to increase. Violence and abuse probably are directly related to emotional buildup in people with no solid, socially accepted ways of relaxing these emotions. Every society needs to provide strong goals of pursuit for the people in it in order to keep that society emotionally relaxed.

The thinking process uses basically three sources from the mind to put together our thought patterns. An idea is triggered from our senses: sight, hearing, smell, taste, and touch. This in turn activates inherited or innate feelings about the subject thought. Then it picks up impressions imprinted early in the formative years and finally current emotional thoughts and feelings. Then we evaluate our idea using all our subconscious material that we have acquired in our life without consciously knowing we had all these feelings and innate, early-imprint, and current subconscious thoughts and then form it into what we feel is a suitable conclusion. We arrive at this conclusion or answer in our reasoning and decision area of the mind, I feel. This area of our mind evaluates all this material sent to it by the subconscious and conscious and makes a decision on it. The brain then sends it to our fully conscious mind where we act on this composite information, not always aware of where all these thoughts or feelings came from. Not only aren't we aware of this subconscious information, but if this early-imprint information is formed under stress and fears early in life, we sometimes can't even control how we act or think when our subconscious fearful thoughts disagree with our emotions. When this happens we become emotionally unstable and can't control our thoughts or actions as we would like. Consistent learned behavior can help correct some of this early-imprint information, but most of the time this information will always influence our thoughts and decisions the rest of our lives. And we will have to learn to live and make decisions despite these abusive subconscious feelings and thoughts we developed. But later learned knowledge we acquired can help if it's similar and positive and comes emotionally through the same area of the subconscious. So basically, therapists can help if they're extremely careful to understand personal emotional feelings completely and don't put in any of their own feelings. Ideas must be strong and supportive so as to strengthen the patient's weak emotional health, thereby turning an emotional weakness into a strength so that he or she can use the emotions to pursue goals to fulfillment. Because through the strengthening of one's pursuits of goals and learning to strive after them brings to your emotions a release of feelings that are hard to live with.

A deceptive and intelligent man covering up his goals, or the type of reasoning or manipulation he is utilizing, does this mostly to keep you from discovering his purposes, because he doesn't always want to disclose his goals to you, feeling you might, due to your natural competitiveness, try to keep him from achieving his purposes. Man will use all kinds of defensive maneuvers to keep others from knowing what he's trying to accomplish, because he mainly doesn't want you to stop or hinder him from accomplishing what he's trying to do, for a man is very defensive because of his competitive nature. This defensiveness and deception is a man's way of going about accomplishing and preserving his goals. Since competitiveness is really made up of two parts, offensive and defensive action, man automatically will employ deceptive cover-up maneuvers to confuse his pursuits. As a football team must include offensive and defensive components, so must a man as he strives after his individual goals. Man doesn't want you to know his goals too well, as he feels subconsciously you might, because of your competitive nature, hinder him from accomplishing his purposes.

Even in our own neighborhoods there is competitiveness at work. It is subtle and doesn't seem like competition, but when a neighbor doesn't strive to keep up his or her house and yard by painting and doing yard work, other neighbors complain to one another. They want their neighbors to work and strive to keep their house and yards neat, as well as to strive to keep their neighborhood clean, orderly, peaceable, and organized. It's somewhat like a football team; they all expect the other members to keep up their part of the team. When they don't, the team falls apart and no one likes to play on the team. The same is true of a neighborhood, when everyone doesn't strive and compete, keeping up their house and yard. The neighborhood falls apart and then no one cares to live there anymore. The neighborhood becomes a slum, with people hating to live there. Competitiveness is necessary in all walks of life; even when it's not easily understood or recognized as competitive, it's there. The competitive spirit is needed in all parts and phases of life to keep man going and mentally healthy and happy. We might desire or want to change some competitive behavior, but we should never just suppress it. What we need to do is find an alternative or better way of competing and encourage that in place of undesirable competitive actions or behavior. For man is naturally competitive and this can't be changed, so let's recognize the potentials of this competitive asset in man.

When sexual emotions are more prevalent in a society, this is due to creative goals not being easily achievable. A society will always turn toward sexual expressions when it is running out of more positive goals. Extreme sexual interests and plenty of social dissent are the last signs and efforts of a society before it ceases to exist. These are really desperate efforts by nature to provide a remnant to survive and indicate a society that is running out of positive creative goals. Most affluent societies will run into this problem when people have more than enough; then that society starts failing, or dying. Once a society has lost its capacity to struggle to survive and has become self-sufficient and affluent, it will become more argumentative and sexual in its lifestyle. A nation must continue to find striving goals of a building type or originating new strong, constructive goals to keep from deteriorating. When a society hasn't enough structuring goals and it becomes affluent, it will always start to fall, for strong goals are needed to keep it alive. To remain strong and keep away from undue social dissent and sexuality, a nation must have strong goals for its people to strive to achieve. Prosperity is death if strong goals disappear. Indications of decay always show signs of sexuality and social bickering. This is, of course, nature's efforts to preserve a natural competitive nature. To get rid of excessive sexual interests and social infighting there is a need for building solid goals with real meaning, which will involve the whole society. If a society will do this, then it will lose its interest in excess sexuality and social fighting. These sexual emotions plus social bickering will fall in the background, and the society will become strong and grow again. For when a society has nothing better to do, it will fight and destroy itself, just like any other natural order. Sometimes societies will decay for a long time, but they will never become strong again until they find strong, interesting goals for their people.

Having goals that you must strive to achieve, not fleeting fun or excitement, is what makes life interesting and enjoyable. We all like to have success or the feeling of having won, but this is only fleeting and soon this feeling will leave and if you don't have another project to start you will start having a letdown feeling. This is normal. To keep oneself from getting this letdown feeling, more goals or projects are needed quickly. Most people think that we should make it as easy as possible for ourselves or our kids, not realizing that the human mind must exert and strive to free itself of pent-up emotions through the competitive process. If we make it easier for ourselves and our family without providing new goals or striving release mechanisms, we are creating a situation that will breed nervousness and turmoil instead. Because by not providing emotional release methods, which are necessary, and by making it easier without providing goals it is not possible for our emotions to relax. This is nature's way for all of life.

In nature there is always a striving taking place in all areas of the world. When these efforts cease, then that area dies. Even flowers strive after sunlight. If they don't receive it because they're too short or are too crowded by taller plants, they wither. The strong and striving in nature make it. Man also is naturally competitive, and when he ceases striving to succeed, he also will die out. So this competitive striving is necessary for man to succeed and have a normal life. Goals in our lives are needed to fulfill a normal existence. Our own society is affluent, and we have more than other societies. But other, less fortunate societies don't have the mental difficulties we have either, because these people have to strive and work just to survive. This is a goal by itself; getting enough to eat and striving hard to live relax their emotions.

Man is born with natural weaknesses and strengths. He must exploit his strengths in goal seeking, using his energies in striving to maintain a normal life. If he takes it easy because his parents or society makes it easy for him, he will not use his natural competitive energies and they will wither or waste away. Man has to strive to survive today, as he has throughout all of history. He cannot change this pattern. He must continue this pattern to maintain his normal emotional balance. You might be irritated by others as they compete with you every day, because you're an emotional being, but as the body depends on a good diet and plenty of exercise to keep disease away, so does our mind need lots of competitive interaction and goal seeking to keep it healthy.

The mind is so constructed that it remains constantly active. Even when you sleep, the mind is mostly repairing itself or dreaming. Dreaming probably is when the mind forms thought patterns for our emotions to use. Since the mind is always busy and likes to remain active, we should realize that relaxing and resting for any length of time are taken negatively by the body and mind. Inactive minds and bodies have a tendency to deteriorate and malfunction. So it is advisable not to rest and sit around or sleep too much. Since man must compete in nature to survive and all of nature follows this rule, then unless everything in nature strives constantly, it falls by the wayside and dies. Man is no exception. Man cannot fight this rule, for we also are a part of nature. Since we follow nature's rules, our mind automatically follows this pattern in its normal functioning, so as to remain healthy. The mind becoming involved in fantasy or unrealistic planning too often will also stop normal competitive interaction and thereby create an abnormal amount of emotional buildup. This, in turn, forces emotional anxiety or forms of depression, because the mind can't handle emotional buildup. Basically, everyday normal striving and interaction are enough in a person's life to keep him or her mentally relaxed, so he or she is okay, but if this person doesn't get enough competitive striving he or she will develop emotional problems. Too much rest and relaxation is not good. What we need are goals and striving after them to fulfill the normal requirements of nature for our mind and body. A therapist who tells you only to rest and relax and tell him your problems is only after your money. He or she might seem nice and relax you a little, but he or she won't do you any good. It would be like a candy or fast-food salesman suggesting you need more of his or her food for a healthy body. What you really need is good basic food and exercise. It's the same with a therapist saying all you need is rest and relaxation. What you really need are competitive goals and good interaction to remain mentally healthy.

The mind is similar to the body as far as getting rid of energy goes. The body must strive and use challenging pursuits to relieve energy as it builds up. To keep strong, it must get rid of the fat. The mind must do the same. After getting rid of extraneous goals, plenty of good goals to pursue will keep the mind healthy and working well. The same as with the body, plenty of good food and exercise will keep the mind healthy. There are lots of technical names for the muscles and fancy names for exercises, but you don't have to know them to exercise and get rid of fat and develop a strong body. The same for the mind. There are plenty of fancy technical names for the emotions and brain, but plenty of good pursuits and reality-based thinking will keep your mind healthy. Knowing fancy vocabulary and technical names for mental illnesses and procedures will get you nothing, so don't try to understand technical data. Don't just sit down or sleep when you feel emotionally upset. This is self-defeating. Pick some nice, solid goals for accomplishing, strive after them, and feel good emotionally right away.

Man is naturally competitive, so the first step to help in the evaluation of a very quiet person, not a seriously mentally ill person, is to determine what his or her goals, if any, are. If there are none, try to determine why. If the person has weak negative goals, how can you go about changing them, so you can help him or her? If the person has weak positive goals, how can you help him or her to achieve more challenging goals? Since goals are basically man's real main purpose and he strives after goals all his life, then mental health must be involved in achieving these goals. Since weak or impossible goals might be involved, should you advise him or her to quit seeking to attain goals, if these goals are causing problems? Not at all. You can help the person change or modify his or her efforts but not quit. For mental illness seems most evident when a person quits, fails, or can't achieve what he or she is trying to do. If he or she stops trying to achieve goals or can't go ahead, the time involved between goals and efforts on his or her part is crucial. The time that is involved between not being able to continue toward a goal and finding another goal is of the utmost importance, for if a person doesn't receive the proper support at this serious time in his or her life, he or she could start developing serious mental difficulties, which would plague him the rest of his or her life. When man competes, he is constantly striving to win at what he's attempting to do, and this is normal. But when a man is failing and does not want to disclose his goal or goals, as he feels that's his private domain, it's difficult to help him. So helping a person who is failing and being defeated and starts becoming depressed is not always easy. For such a person will sometimes hide his or her goals, which he or she is not achieving for different reasons of his or her own, and not always tell enough of the circumstances surrounding his or her failures but become defensive. Then when you try and help such a person you can't, because he or she won't accept your help, as that would mean disclosing failures and weaknesses. You can't understand this person's real goals, which he or she is hiding because of guilt and defensive feelings, and in turn this makes this person reject your support, because it doesn't meet his or her needs. For a man will not accept just any goal for his life. It must satisfy his personal emotional needs. Since time is crucial, the best way to help him is to strongly support and urge other goals for his life, for with your doing this often he will then disclose his real and hidden goals and bring them out in the open. So then you can suggest and advise him on what he should do so as to continue, if possible, seeking out his real goals and interests. If it's not possible for him to continue, then what are his next best options or goals for his life? For he must go ahead with positive goals to fulfill his needs to express himself or fall by the wayside, as so many are doing now. Striving after goals is the only thing that will keep a man mentally healthy. A man will learn anything he needs to learn or do to accomplish his goals. This is man's nature, so encourage him to keep trying and not give in to opposition or failure if he feels his goals are worthwhile. Sometimes support, active or quiet, is all that is needed for him to continue and succeed at what he should accomplish. As far as the seriously mentally ill person goes, this is not for him or her, although it would help the person to get on goals of some kind, helped by a trained therapist. For goals will help even severely mentally ill patients to feel some emotional relaxation. Some will get along better with their peers and be accepted more.

Some thought patterns we have developed in our early life will not suffice now to release our emotional levels and will sometimes, if circumstances in our everyday life become too troubling, cause an emotional imbalance. Our emotions will conflict with what we want to do, and if we persist in trying to do what our emotions object to, we will suffer turmoil and depression and sometimes it will immobilize us. So innate emotional brain stimuli, plus early-imprint, formative information and everyday thought patterns must agree to some degree before your mind can act intelligently and reasonably. If your mind tries to act without consent of your emotions, it will show up in your actions, in indecision and negative behavior. When others cause irritations by hindering you or objecting to what you are trying to accomplish, this will also cause emotional discomfort to you. These actions will hinder and interfere with decision making on your part and keep you from achieving your goals. If this interference or hindering and irritations from others is enough to stop you, this will cause emotional buildups in you. So try to not let other people interfere or stop you in your efforts, for our minds are naturally goal-oriented to accomplish or succeed in everything we do. So don't take irritations so seriously that they stop you. This could be devastating. Failing in our pursuits, with no chance of continuing our goals and efforts, is taken very negatively by our competitive minds, as this always causes emotional turmoil. So if you do fail, for some reason, don't quit. Find similar goals and start again. For negative emotional failures have a tendency to follow and stay in our conscious minds until we have had some success in that area before we can reach emotional peace. Our mind is naturally competitive and goal-oriented and this cannot be altered, so we must live within these limitations or fall by the wayside. In other words, don't let people stop you from pursuing goals. You may have to become defensive or continue arguing quietly, but keep on. Don't stop pursuing your goals. Your emotional health is at stake.

Basically, our ego or self-image is attacked when depression hits. Our self-esteem is drastically involved, sometimes almost destroyed, when we become depressed. Maybe we should consider this consequence when we stop another person from fulfilling his or her goals. Try being constructive instead of being critical of another's goals. Before criticizing too much, try ways of supporting the goal. Since depression attacks an important subconscious area of our minds, be careful when hindering or causing irritation to another, because you don't realize the serious damage that could occur if that person feels he or she is a complete failure and becomes depressed. When a person's inner self-worth is gone, it is very difficult to get that person competitive or wanting to strive after goals again. So the more often a man fails, the lower his self-esteem or self-image becomes and the less he wants to try accomplishing or seeking emotion-releasing goals again. So this is detrimental to mental well-being. If you feel you must be critical, finish up by being supportive and encouraging, for making a person fail and become depressed is nothing to be proud of.

Depression seems to be more evident and detrimental as a person's energy level decreases. When a person's confidence or self-esteem falls, he or she is more susceptible to depression, which makes an impression on mental actions. So a person with good feelings or emotions about him- or herself will be affected less by failures than a person who felt down already. Try to keep people from feeling emotionally negative, and there will be less chance of a depressive illness. Supporting and encouraging people as they strive after goals, not letting irritations stop them, is the best form of therapy or preventive help. And so try to keep a fairly high emotional level for yourself and those around you so as to prevent emotional problems. Surround yourself with pursuits and goals that keep you not only busy, but content. Try to enjoy what you are doing. It will help you. Always among all your goals that you are striving after keep some interesting and enjoyable goals. This will help keep up your self-esteem, a needed asset in life.

When people develop depression and difficulties making decisions that creates serious consequences for their emotions. A person making a decision starts a mental process of going ahead with pursuit of a goal or some other objective purpose. If he or she fails in his or her pursuit, it creates more guilt feelings. Now if the person has a low rate of success in life in reaching goals, that means a higher rate of failure, and failure to reach a goal always brings into the mind or emotions guilt and depressive feelings, and this is normal but difficult to live with. For the mind is goal-oriented to succeed, not to fail. So when a person starts failing, feelings of failure and depression start creeping in, which no one can live with. This occurs because the mind actually uses depressive emotions to try to force a stronger competitive striving, so as to get you to strive for your goals and succeed. But if you don't have a strong background of learned thought patterns that will help you achieve your goals, you will probably fail, unless you can get help from others. The more you fail and get these strong depressive feelings, the less you are going to feel like making any more decisions or trying to achieve new goals, because the depressive feelings are so terrible to handle. So success breeds success and failure breeds failure, as the saying goes. And failure is not easy for a person to live with. So your telling a person to keep on making decisions and trying won't be accepted very easily by a person who fails a lot and knows how he or she feels when that happens.

Sometimes we feel irritations cause depression. You could say they do, indirectly. Irritations cause a person hindrances so as to prevent him or her from pursuing goals. Then this failure in not being able to pursue goals activates depressive emotions in his or her mind. For depression is an emotion used by the mind to force us to go on despite the irritations or hindrances that are occurring. The fact that our energy level seems to drop as irritations occur make us feel this is the main reason for depression. The mind always will use a lot more energy when irritations or hindrances occur while we are trying to continue seeking our objectives. That is why we connect irritations to depression, but really as our energy runs out, the mind still wants to achieve its goal and this triggers our depressive emotions. Because the mind is goal-oriented, as soon as the energy level drops depressive emotions start so as to keep the competitive action going. Then, as irritations deplete our energy, the brain uses depressive energies to overcome the irritations and hindrances. When the brain starts using more depressive emotions to keep you moving forward toward your objectives, it is so failures do not stop you from

75

achieving your goal. To stop striving toward one's objectives or goals when hindrances or irritations happen could be devastating. Even though you feel depressive emotions at times, strive harder. This will relax those emotions. That is why the mind uses these feelings to force you to continue toward your goals. I have heard concentration camp and POW camp survivors say that the people who gave in to these terrible feelings and got depressed did not make it. Those who tried harder lost those depressive feelings, due to their striving, to accomplish their purpose, to make it, and they often did. They never let these terrible feelings stop them. So do not let irritations or depressive feelings stop you. Use these feelings to make you strive harder to succeed. Remember then that irritations do bring on depressed feelings, but only as you run out of your normal energy. The only time you should worry is when there are enough irritations to stop you. If this happens, the depressive feelings will come on in full force.

So do not let irritations stop you. Ignore them as much as you can and/or start striving after new goals. Stopping for any length of time can be devastating, as depressive feelings will increase rapidly. If depressive feelings happen to you, do not be alarmed. Just realize they are normal. Everyone has them at times, and they are meant to motivate you on toward your objectives.

It seems there are designated areas of the brain where certain impulses of solid direction have been imprinted. Around these solid impulse centers, depending on amount of interest, are areas of the brain that develop and support these impulse centers. Support areas develop around these impulse centers in order to give dimension and add learned information to these areas so our conscious mind can think, and act more efficiently. As these support areas around these impulse centers develop, depending on size they can add greatly to what we want to do actively within a given discipline. We might have a talent, but until that area around that talent impulse center becomes developed we never will use our potential to its fullest. The mind has to have inherited in it the basic concept before development can occur. These solid information centers are innate, but early-imprint materials add to it greatly. This imprint material is only developed in specific areas of the mind, developed for this purpose. If you didn't have specific innate material imprinted you couldn't exercise or develop this talent in the immediate surrounding tissue of the brain or bring it to physical reality. Other life must also have these solid imprint centers through inherited means before they can develop; otherwise they can go no further in actions than the imprint centers have developed. That's what limits human actions as well as actions of other forms of life and living matter; they all possess inherited imprinted areas of the mind. Without these inherited, innate, imprinted guidance and direction centers we couldn't develop at all, and without development areas around each innate area we couldn't change or do anything different. So we need everything we inherited in order to think or do anything that we're able to do. We can advance or change only as much as the area immediately surrounding these imprint areas will allow us. No life can advance or do more in any direction than these areas allow. Even the diversity allowed, due to the surrounding brain tissue, is governed and limited to a certain extent. As in a plant, when something hinders its normal growth it will be able to modify its shape somewhat, but only within limitations, the same is true of our intellect.

All emotions use the competitive grid system of our mind in order for release. Since this is the only way our emotions are expressed, it is necessary that we develop proper competitive expression that is compatible with others. We say some people grate on our nerves; this means they have developed offensive, noncompatible ways that are unacceptable to others in society. There is an old saying: "When in Rome, do as the Romans do"; this means if you want to get along and accomplish something, use acceptable behavior patterns. You will be able to accomplish what you want to do more easily and not be confronted by resistance or defensive actions. So try to develop proper attitudes so people will not resist or oppose you, and you can more easily accomplish your goals.

We must use our competitive grid system in order to express our emotions, and we have to express these emotions to have a normal life. We must be able to accomplish this before we can relax and start renewing our energy levels. Emotional buildup is damaging to live with, as our emotions demand expression or anxiety and/or depression will set in. Sometimes we are our own worst enemy, because when our emotions build up due to irritations and we're using up all our energies, we start acting aggressive toward others. This action is unacceptable, so they object and resist our attitude and oppose us and reject us further. This, in turn, doesn't allow us to express our built-up emotions, due to irritations happening, and the result is not being able to release the emotions we must release to keep relaxed. So teach yourself to control your defensive hostile feelings so you can continue to accomplish your goals and in the process relieve your emotions. Stronger, prevalent emotions start influencing our actions when there is a lack of normal everyday goals to relax them. When there is a lack of goals by which we can release normal emotions, then stronger emotions start influencing our thoughts in order to force and motivate us toward pursuing stronger goals in order to release emotional buildup. The mind will not allow the emotions to build up without turning to different emotional processes to get the mind moving and the thought process continuing. The mind is always active; it never shuts down. There are always thought processes taking place. Any outside influence or stimulus that triggers thought will also trigger the appropriate emotions, and these emotions are conveyed through use of the natural competitive grid system. Man is naturally competitive and uses this system to transform his thoughts into actions. Different thoughts as they are formulated in the mind are utilized subtly or actively to formulate defensive or offensive patterns. Since this is done subconsciously, we're not aware of this process until we evaluate what we are trying to achieve or accomplish. Then obvious patterns of defensive and offensive maneuvers can be observed as thoughts are transformed into action. Exercising and using our emotions is the only way we can have a normal life. This is understood somewhat, but how to accomplish it is not, and just expressing ourselves verbally will not do it, especially if we have been irritated strongly by someone, because hard feelings and resentment toward others do create strong guilt feelings in our minds and verbalizing or talking about it doesn't help us with any long-lasting relief. We must develop striving goals. We're so subtle in the way we do things in setting up goals and trying to achieve our objectives and this is competitive, but because it's in our subconscious we're not aware of it being done. So by striving after things we want and would like we are expanding competitive energies even though we're not aware of it. Since these are normal actions for all people, people accept this behavior in others and expect it unconsciously without noticing it. Also, it's the normal way to release our emotions and find normal mental health and well-being releasing emotional pressure through this method. So the release of competitive energies with our emotions is so subtle you have to analyze all expression carefully to see and understand how it's accomplished. When you're thinking or planning quietly, you will use offensive or defensive ways of obtaining these goals or objectives. All our thinking is used and developed for the purpose of obtaining goals, or things we want to accomplish. This seeking after things or trying to accomplish purposes that interest us takes competitive energies on our part to be able to achieve. This is done subtly, subconsciously, and we're not even aware that we are using our competitive emotions to obtain these things.

Some people feel only offensive actions are competitive, and when you indicate that people are continuously competitive they don't understand. But defensive actions are just as much a part of football, baseball, or any other competitive action as offensive maneuvers. So people in very subtle ways will do things to place another on the defensive; this then allows them to act offensively. But there are times when defensive maneuvers are used by people subconsciously, using this action to get a proper offensive response in another person. Women will often act coy, very feminine, and resistant, holding back, with the conscious intent of getting a certain man interested personally in them. This is a defensive act. It in turn triggers man's offensive feelings to pursue and try to achieve a conquest, a man's offensive feelings are stimulated by a woman using different enticing defensive resistance maneuvers. Even though a woman is aware consciously that she's doing this, leading a man to be interested in her, still a lot of these actions she uses are subconsciously, defensively, incited.

Since a man enjoys being on the offensive, because this gives him a better chance to express his emotions, he will often take advantage of a defensive posture in another. Since this is a quite normal way to feel when they're competitive, people sometimes believe the only time they're being competitive is when they're acting on the offensive. But truthfully, you are being competitive even when you are feeling negative and forced into a defensive attitude or even if you use it unwillingly. This also is the other half of competitive action not relished by people, as they often don't like the feelings they have when in a defensive position. But since this is part of competitive interaction it must be included in our view of this important behavior between people. How you handle your feelings when placed in a defensive position by others is crucial in determining how successfully you get along in life. If you refuse to get into a defensive position and only want to be on the offensive with others, you will find yourself in an untenable situation and probably be rejected more than you would like. So learning how to be defensive in a normal or polite way and in a courteous manner is worth thinking about and practicing intelligently, as it will often help you. Also, if you are low on energy, tired, and depressed, it is harder to be on the defensive, as this position takes more energy than being in an offensive position, but it is part of the competitive attitude in man's daily actions, some defensive and some offensive behaviors, a constant interaction throughout the day. Some people are too defensive in their actions due to depression and low levels of energy; this will cause problems in normal interaction, so we should take this into consideration when interacting with others. Encouraging offensive action on their part and helping develop this trait in them will benefit them and ourselves both. Some people are very good being placed in a defensive position and have developed certain actions that help them do this. We enjoy being around them, as we can use our offensive feeling more and this we enjoy. So think about allowing yourself to be put in a defensive attitude with others at times in an intelligent way, and this will help your position with others, you will be accepted more, be a good listener, with proper responses, not hostile ones, and you will develop better methods to release your own emotions offensively.

Also, remember that repeated irritations are probably the cause of most depression and other mental problems. By using the correct methods in seeking to achieve our objectives or goals we can prevent unnecessary irritations and depression. This will keep us from getting a series of irritations that can hinder or stop us from proceeding toward our goals, for stopping us from achieving our goals is taken very badly by our goal-seeking minds, as we are constantly trying to achieve what interests us. Also, any support or effort by others to help us achieve our conquest or goals is appreciated. But if it hinders our efforts of conquest or goals it is taken very badly by the mind. Irritations and hindrances often cause anxiety and depression in adults and mental problems in young children. But correction or helping to achieve our goals is not taken negatively by the mind but positively, and the person receiving the correction will have positive feelings about it and you. So all interference is not received the same way. If it supports a person's efforts it may be taken well, and if it hinders his or her efforts it may be taken very badly by the mind. I've seen strong correction taken very well and strong correction taken badly, depending on if it supported the person's goals or not. Take, for instance, a coach of a sports team. He or she will use harsh discipline at times and it actually may encourage his or her team, because it helps them achieve their objective. Any strong organization will use discipline to achieve success, and it often won't be used detrimentally by the people involved. But at times it will; if it stops a person from achieving his or her goal, the effects could be disastrous. All correction should be evaluated. Ask yourself this question: Will it encourage a person or will it stop him or her from going ahead with his or her objectives and goals? If it will encourage the person and help him or her meet his or her goals, good! If it stops him or her from achieving his or her objectives, it is very damaging. Most of our emotional problems are caused by improper correction.

If you're not finding plenty of sufficient goals to relieve your emotions, as the mind uses this competitive process to release your emotions, you're in trouble. For the emotions firing up and sending out stimuli into the mind that are not released through the proper process will cause emotional problems for a person. The emotions must be expressed, so the mind will use different processes to try to accomplish this action. If it is not accomplished, the negative actions from that person will be expressed because of a buildup of emotions and people will reject this attitude. So we must find suitable ways to accomplish this. For if we're rejected because of our bad negative attitude, we won't be able to release our emotions. Since releasing our emotions is essential for mental health, we must cultivate proper behavior in order to do this. A bad negative attitude will not help us to express ourselves. We must find better ways of expression, so others will interact positively with us and our objectives will not be hindered, so we can accomplish this necessity of life. I notice that good therapists often will do this for their patients, finding acceptable goals, without knowing fully why, just that it helps their patients emotionally. These therapists will help patients find goals or objectives and use proper steps for teaching them how to go about accomplishing these goals, not fully realizing why they're doing this. But even if they're not completely aware why they're doing this, they're doing exactly what is needed to help people back on their feet. But it's often hit-or-miss, and many therapists, not being fully aware of the importance of this procedure, not understanding all the ramifications, do not accomplish enough. Even the ones that use goals primarily as treatment don't understand their importance to mental health and don't emphasize them the right way. We should weed out useless negative therapy, which doesn't help, and concentrate only on positive methods of support. Making people aware of what will help and what won't help them back to normal mental health should be everyone's objective, not the wishy-washy systems we use today. For therapists use so many different methods of therapy, many aren't helpful and some methods contribute to lasting mental difficulties.

Our goals, as they're stimulated by our thoughts, are always influenced by our emotions. We pick most goals purely to satisfy our emotions and express our feelings. Even though we express our emotions through our competitive grid system, our emotions influence us to choose the type of goal we wili use. So our goals indicate what emotions are being stimulated the most and how our emotions often dictate our goals to be expressed. This is how we find relief, expressing ourselves through goals that express certain emotions we feel. Our thoughts stimulate our emotions, and once they're stimulated they must be expressed or there will be trouble generated in the mind until they are released.

We must express our emotional needs, which we have due to learned-imprint data or current emotional feelings as they are stimulated. Understanding these needs and expressing them so they won't cause undue emotional turmoil is the only way to maintain mental balance. But these needs must be expressed in the way they're intended to be expressed or we won't feel fulfillment. Discovering the way we have to follow to fulfill our needs is necessary to reach a satisfied emotional state. Expressing our needs any way we feel like will not accomplish these results. The proper personal interaction and natural resistance needed to get the desired result for our emotions to feel relaxed is what we have to have to feel normal. Unless our needs and emotions receive the necessary resistance as we express them, they cannot relax or be fulfilled. Because striving is part of life on earth and all of life is involved, we are not exempt; we either participate in the struggle of life or fall by the wayside.

Ordinary friendships are formed because of people

with similar interests seeking the same objectives. As a person interacts with another person, one of the two will be on the defensive and the other will be on the offensive, as there are two parts to competitive interaction. This defensive and offensive interaction will swing back and forth between the two people; first one, then the other will take position or the other. People form friends by interacting defensively or offensively with them and observing how each handles these parts of competitive interaction when they converse. You either win or lose with people as you interact with them; you make friends or lose them depending on how you feel emotionally. When you are placed in too defensive or offensive a position as you interact, you won't make friends with that person because you will feel uncomfortable. When you find common pursuits and compatible people emotionally you won't feel defensive and you will make friends, as the competitive release you feel subconsciously will urge you to make friends. Societies must have solid growth goals to eliminate petty arguing in their midst because of strong prevalent emotions, like self-preservation and sexuality, arguing, murder on TV and on the streets, plus different sexual deviations taking place. So social goals must be compatible with benefits to the society and involve all of the society. Releasing emotions through common goals is the only way a society can be content and relaxed. Finding proper goals is the means to a well-ordered and happy society.

4

Why Is Man Competitive?

No competitive system is only offensive, as all competitive action has two parts, offensive and defensive. Even though we're primarily interested in our offensive capacity, as our minds relax by this means, we also need to understand the importance defensive situations have in this important action. There must always be defensive reactions to get the proper response to our offensive needs. Defensive action is always needed to get our offensive drives to be realized fully and must provide the proper resistance to be effective. We must be fully aware of defensive situations to benefit from their effect on our offensive-oriented minds, which only relax when we rid ourselves of emotional buildups this way. Defensive situations are so important that we should spend thoughtful time planning and making sure defensive situations are resistant enough to relieve our emotions. For the mind will not relax unless it gets the defensive response necessary in order to trigger our emotions to release their energies. Often we view defensive situations negatively because we think of all the effort that we're going to have to expend to overcome them, not realizing the benefits we actually are getting from striving to overcome and that we're actually releasing different emotions that keep us mentally relaxed. This natural dislike of defensive objectives is often hard to overcome and could cause emotional difficulties if we give in to this weakness and do not strive ahead. So try to find hard goals to strive to achieve, which you like, and not be stopped by goals you don't like attempting to achieve. Try not to view defensive objectives too negatively, even if you don't like them. If you have to achieve them, look at them as positively as you can and strive to accomplish these objectives and you will be more comfortable emotionally because of it. If you don't have other defensive objectives to strive against to relieve your emotions, you could be asking for tensions to build in your mind and they will stop you. So view defensive situations with a positive attitude, and you'll be further ahead. Don't expect defensive goals to be exciting—most of the time they're not—the benefits derived must be viewed, knowing that the reward for better emotions will be well worth the efforts. So very often defensive pursuits look very negative, especially if we're a little down or depressed, but emotionally there is a reward if we just go ahead. For a while I considered not including defensive examples in this book, as our minds are not defensively oriented, but I thought it might provide some understanding of our competitive natures. Therefore, try to view defensive resistant objectives not according to how you feel about them, for often you will feel that they're distasteful and burdensome. Look at them positively, as objectives you're going to conquer, and you will benefit emotionally if you do. I will not illustrate how distastefully we sometimes view resistant defensive pursuits, just the value and benefit they provide for our emotions. I'll just write how defensiveness affects our minds in a mechanical way, not all the feelings of objection they might bring.

The first part of my book did not explain the defensive structuring of our human competitive system. This chapter will deal primarily with defensive situations and how defense fulfills our competitive need. People don't often think about that part of competitive action that is defensiveness. Since this takes up much of competitive action, we should learn to recognize this part of competitive interaction. In man's striving, he constantly uses competitive energies. Anything that he strives against automatically becomes a defensive force. This means anything that requires force, on his part, to overcome it. So a mountain could become a defensive force if we tried to climb it, or anything else we're striving to overcome that requires concentration on our part to accomplish. Very often we argue and force people around us to become defensive toward us as we try to get them to see things our way and they resist us. This resistance often will get us to argue and strive harder to convince the other so we can see both sides, offensive and defensive, as competitive action is displayed—offensive action on your part, as you strive to convince the other person of your ideas, and defensive action on the other's part, as he or she resists your opinions, because most people view things differently. This arguing forms the defensive resistance we need to release our competitive emotions, although our mind only uses its offensive action in order to release emotions. Since offensive actions release our emotions, and not defensive actions, we tend to be offensively inclined. So our emotions, as they're released, will give off a feeling of well-being in our minds and since we enjoy feeling good, we tend to be on the offensive more than defensive in our attitude. But since defensive action is so much a part of competitive actions, we should realize that how we act defensively when we're put in that position should be of the utmost importance to us. Acting too defensive and resistant toward another could cause overall rejection by that person you're trying to communicate with, therefore causing tension to both individuals involved, to some extent. So all resistance and attitudes of defensiveness toward others should always be tempered and controlled on your part to keep from causing undue emotional restraint in others and yourself. For the releasing of one's emotions can only happen when defensive resistance occurs in the proper amount to provide opposition but not stop another completely. If it stops another person's emotional expression completely, then the only thing that happens is that person's emotions will build up and cause tension in his or her mind. The best defensive actions put up resistance but never inhibit the other completely. Some people learn defensive actions well and use them so effectively that people like to be around them, for they know that person will never put them down permanently but will interact with them and encourage them to try harder. For no one wants to be put down hard; it's too difficult to get started again and if it happens too often we have a tendency to quit and not try anymore. Then our emotions and tensions build up, due to a lack of striving on our part, and depression is left. So always try to keep this in mind when dealing with others. Just don't stop them, but guide and encourage with forethought and better resistance patterns on your part so the other will be able to continue more effectively toward his or her goals. For the striving after goals releases our emotions and makes for feelings of well-being in our minds. Therefore, others will like you because you helped them continue when they interacted with you and this made them feel emotionally satisfied. But letting yourself be put in a defensive position might not make you feel good, as defensive feelings are not something we like to have. When we feel defensive we also feel uncomfortable, as we would rather be in an offensive, striving state, as this releases our emotions. But often we can't help being put in a defensive emotional state, due to circumstances around us, so we should learn more about these feelings and how to work with these defensive emotions of ours.

A football team has a proper defensive part, and the better they learn defensive maneuvers, the more they help their team. The same with us—we all have to be in defensive positions at times, so the more we learn about how to handle this part of our competitive life, the better we will help ourselves and others. The main thing to learn when put in a defensive position is not to get *too* defensive and upset over it. Control your emotions, because though you naturally won't like this negative position, remember that if you handle the defensive position well, you will probably help yourself when it's your turn in the offensive situation. For people have a tendency to allow you as much courtesy as you gave them when they were striving to present their opinions to you. So when you're on the defense in interaction with another, don't stop that person roughly. Be considerate, even encouraging, and let that person state his or her opinions. Then he or she will have better feelings toward you as he or she releases emotions when presenting opinions while conversing with you. If you stopped the person, his or her emotions would build up, causing frustration. As frustration builds, anger will come out, so try not to stop a person from presenting his or her thoughts to you, though this will take learning and understanding on your part. So even if you feel extremely defensive, due to someone's offensive attitude toward you, and this will create resentful feelings in you, learn to handle these feelings intelligently and not let them control you. Defensive feelings are probably the hardest emotions to handle intelligently, because we don't like them. When we feel these emotional frustrations we have to control them so they don't cause undue harm to us and others around us. Defensive, hostile feelings often arise quickly, so learn proper defensive maneuvering, coaching yourself over a period of time so when placed in a bad defensive position you won't lose your cool. Remember, everyone gets placed in defensive positions, so don't get overly upset, for the better you handle defensive feelings, the more you will succeed with others. A great deal of interaction with others will automatically place you in bad defensive situations, so be resistant, but not overly so.

The relationship between men and women demonstrates competitive interactions very well and how offensive and defensive actions contribute to positive lifestyles. Women act and dress in a positive way; as pretty flowers attract bees, so do pretty women attract men. Women naturally try to dress well and look nice, mainly to attract men. Competing with other women in their efforts to look nice, they evaluate their looks by what others are wearing in their efforts to attract favorable attention. This effort is positive, so you would list this effort as offensive competitive action on their part. Then come the desired effects, as men are attracted by these efforts. Then something strange takes place. Men, when they're attracted by women's careful efforts, use positive, offensive actions in their pursuit, but something different happens in women. Since you can't have two offensive efforts at the same time, a woman almost at the moment she attracts a man in a positive manner starts defensively resisting his efforts. This seems unnatural because of all the positive efforts she at first displayed trying to attract the man. But since the offensive efforts of the man must have defensive action to make competitive actions complete, a woman starts becoming more resistant as she feels his attention increasing. So the harder he tries, the more she makes him strive to "catch" her, thus fulfilling this natural phenomenon of competitive action, which relaxes man's emotions but also helps a woman indirectly. Women often comment that they don't understand themselves. First they're trying hard to attract a man, and as soon as they do they subconsciously start resisting him. But since emotions are intertwined or released through offensive and defensive competitive interaction, this is natural and benefits both parties, and since competitive interaction must use defensive as well as offensive action, it is completely normal to interact this way. Then the question comes up: If defensive actions aren't as desirable as offensive actions, as these don't provide emotional release, why do women do this defensive action? It seems attracting a man must somehow allow her a chance to become offensive, for release of her emotions in a positive way is also necessary. This she mainly does by trying to attract a man she will like and feels is emotionally strong, who will accept her and interact with her strongly but not abusively. So she wants to act positively with him, not in a defensive attitude but as a strong, resistant, but courteous individual.

So you can see a woman subconsciously is willing to go through all these efforts to attract and to get a strong individual who won't abuse her, but still one who she can respect and interact positively with. This is her way of finding competitive emotional release in a marriage, not through attracting but positive interaction afterward.

Also, a woman will reject a man if she is being pursued too hard and will become extremely uncomfortable and desperate as she becomes more defensive, because under no circumstances can you feel good when being too defensive. You will always feel slightly down when resisting others. We only do it to help our chances to be on the offensive and be able to pursue goals we should like to work at. So defensive resistance is a necessary evil as far as your emotions go, but often very beneficial if you can evaluate and possibly see openings or chances for you to achieve positive goals of your own.

Men often notice a natural resistance in women, and this seems to attract them. This resistance is often misunderstood by men. They sometimes don't know whether it only means for them to pursue harder or to leave the woman alone and get lost. So men often pursue a woman when the woman really means no and doesn't want the man's attention.

Since defensive actions are not consciously sought because of the negative feeling they develop in our brain, we won't automatically get involved, but subconsciously we know that if done properly, defensive actions trigger an offensive response in the one we're interested in interacting with.

This action often causes a woman, when she knows she is striving to catch the right man and finds him, to automatically subconsciously become defensive. She can't figure out what makes her change so abruptly, not always knowing that to get an offensive response she must provide the proper defensive attitude to make the male pursue her. She will sometimes wonder why is she becoming defensive, since no one automatically becomes defensive, so it might be innate. If she has to become overly defensive, this will make her worried and then begin creating fear, because no one can become too defensive without the emotions starting to begin rejecting an untenable relationship.

The difference that occurs when a woman who is trying to attract a man starts feeling she is attracting him is almost felt subconsciously. The need to continue to attract and at the same time resist his efforts in order to continue to draw forth more offensive efforts from him is almost subconsciously initiated. As she still feels the need to attract him, her subconscious knows that to increase his desire she has to resist his efforts. So she attracts and resists almost simultaneously in her efforts not to lose his interest. Women often feel they're not being defensive when they're trying to get the man they're after interested and pursuing them, but they are. It is the same as an army defending itself creating a weakness in their defensive lines so as to get the opposing army to break through in attack, then ambushing them. A woman also makes weakness in her defenses for the man she's interested in to catch her, and when he breaks through she's got him. She must provide defensive situations to challenge his offensive efforts at pursuit; the difference is that when he falls into her ambush she lets him catch her. After he's caught her he will then provide resistance toward her emotions. Sometimes a woman actually knows she is attempting to trap a man by offensively trying to attract him and defensively getting him to pursue her. This combination of offensive and defensive moves is most often carried out quite subconsciously, but defensively competitive action is used in her efforts. The harder she tries to catch a man, the more her emotions relax, because she will always seek a compatible personality and one that resists her and makes her try harder to please him emotionally is the one she wants.

If a person doesn't marry for love, he or she must find positive resistance in other ways to get emotional release. This can occur in any strong challenge or pursuit, for only in the release of our emotions through offensive and defensive competitive efforts do we feel comfortable in life. When you put up with others too often and feel reserved when conversing and interacting with people, you're in a defensive situation. You do not enjoy this part of competitiveness, as it does not allow you to express your emotions freely, but when you're on the positive offensive initiative you do enjoy it. But to get along with others you should learn how to handle yourself when placed in a restrictive situation, as they will like you more if they can interact freely with you in both an offensive and a defensive position.

Defensive action is the most difficult part of competitive interaction. No one likes to be on the defensive, as it gets you down. Defensive feelings are always negative, so when you feel down and reserved when conversing and interacting you're not succeeding, as your mind feels depressed. When you feel positive and are striving and succeeding in achieving goals you're on the offensive and you will feel good. Our minds are set up to work at succeeding, and we feel good when we're accomplishing objectives. When stopped or delayed, we start feeling defensive and down. So we naturally tend to strive after goals as often as we can and this creates positive stimuli that enter our brain through our emotions. Still, defensive feelings are as much a part of competitive action as offensive action, so we have to learn about this facet of our emotions to get along. We must learn to play by new rules when feeling defensive and down when dealing with others and only be cautiously defensive so as to continue the relationship and pursuits within better limitations. Sometimes, even in very defensive relationships, there will often develop worthwhile offensive pursuits through which we can release lots of emotions, thereby creating strong positive feelings in our minds. For only when we can express our emotions positively can we feel good about everything, and then minor hindrances and problems won't affect our positive self-image. So resistance toward others should be handled carefully, because you don't know if it will lead to positive goals for you to pursue.

So as you feel resistance in someone you're talking or working with, remember that this is a natural defensive mechanism of a competitive reaction, which always takes place. This reaction is natural, and you can't help notice, if you start looking for it, a normal competitive resistance as you interact with others. This resistance, depending on the conversation, always means a form of competitive interaction is taking place. *Positive* means offensive action and *negative* a defensive attitude. This innate subconscious action always takes place as you interact with others. Notice this competitive interaction between men and women, as it illustrates positive moves by women being resisted by men and positive action by men being resisted by women in this natural interaction. This is so natural and normal we don't even think about it, just accept it. It varies between men and women, as all people are different, but basically it's similar, this competitive resistance and positive action most of the time.

So we go through life resisting or being positive toward everything that happens to us; this is our innate competitive instinct. Whenever you can see resistance in someone you're conversing with or feel resistance in yourself as you converse, you're recognizing a defensive action. This hinders your natural offensive inclination to move forward. So only when you're using your emotions in an offensive, positive effort do you get a good feeling and know your emotions are expressing themselves in a positive way and all is well. Know also that when you see others being resistant and quiet they are not releasing emotional energies and therefore will develop tension and possibly forms of depression if their minds stay in a defensive, inactive state.

Then, if resistance forms a defensive situation that a person might use to struggle against and release emotions in an offensive manner, why isn't any resistance okay? Because of personal interests, each person has different likes and dislikes and will seek out something that interests him or her and only then will he or she strive after it. If it doesn't interest a person, he or she won't go after or pursue any goal, even though any goal will help get rid of emotional tensions. So we must at times support people in finding goals by which to release tensions if they personally can't find ones that interest them in going ahead. If people become depressed, it is harder and sometimes impossible for them to motivate themselves to find goals that interest them. Then a trained therapist is needed to help motivate them by determining what they like and are capable of accomplishing, because failure-oriented and depressed people don't want to try because they feel they can't succeed. They must be helped carefully to get over this feeling and must be shown that they can succeed and find emotional release. As they find release from their emotions, they will start accomplishing small goals on their own and become motivated to seek other pursuits for themselves. When a person is depressed, he or she is not conscious and capable of understanding what his or her problems really are and what to do about them. If he or she did know, he or she wouldn't have a problem. No one likes depressive feelings. Often a depressed person becomes very defensive and quiet due to his or her effort to protect him- or herself from what he or she feels others are trying to do to him or her. Advice is taken negatively by depressed people because they feel the advice won't work and they really don't have enough energy to do anything anyway. His or her energies are being used mostly by confusion and feelings of failure over different things that have happened to him or her.

Since most of these failures are overly magnified, these overwhelm the decision process and sap all a person's energies. So trying to motivate a person toward goals is difficult and requires lots of personal information, as the person will resist and become more defensive, thus using up more energies. As he or she resists advice and energy drops, he or she feels more depressed and blames it on the advice, even though it was caused by his or her resistant, negative defensiveness. So we dislike being defensive, as it saps our energies, but at times we will be placed in defensive spots that, if we learn how to handle them, can help us reach goals of our own. As a football team has a defensive unit, so do most interactions among people. You have to become defensive at times to interact. If you do it correctly, you can get your chance to be on the offensive side much more as you learn how to be defensive correctly. Therefore, defensive maneuvering should be thought out carefully because of the opportunities that could be opened as you interact. Proper actions by the defensive unit of a football team will give the offensive team more of a chance to score when they get the football.

Some people do a better job interacting with others they oppose and are more supportive even when they're resisting a person's opinions. This tendency to support people even when disagreeing is taken very well by our emotions, and we generally get along better and become friends quickly because of it. Resisting others to the point of stopping their efforts is taken very negatively by the emotions, but resistance with support actually strengthens our own efforts. Anyone who supports our goals, even through using strong correction toward us, is taken positively by our competitive emotions. But if we feel the other person is being too negative and trying unduly to stop our efforts, we tend to dislike him or her. So it's best, even when another person is being too offensive, not to reject and stop that person—just resist and correct him or her, but still support him or her if at all possible. If you have to stop these efforts, then quickly try to get that person started on new goals; otherwise his or her emotions will start giving him or her trouble. No one can have his or her competitive energies stopped for any length of time without serious emotional problems developing. A man can use anything, even a mountain, for a defensive opponent. Because anything he strives to conquer or overcome is a challenge to him, something that makes him work hard to win will use his competitive energies. Since a man must strive constantly to accomplish almost everything he does, competitive energies are involved indirectly in almost everything.

Opposition and resistance toward you are normal in defensive or offensive opportunities occurring as you go through life. People often feel everyone is out to get them or oppose them and keep them from accomplishing what they're trying to do. Since all of nature, including man, is striving and competing, these people are right. Man's fear of failure and the emotional consequences makes him try harder to strive and succeed at all his goals. When you feel strong resistance as you come in contact with someone, maybe it's because that person is placing you in a defensive attitude, and so you wonder what the other person is thinking about. Also, you don't like to tell others about your weaknesses and feelings of inferiority because you feel they might use these things against you later when interacting with you. We have a tendency to show only our best side toward others and try not to give them more opportunities to learn our weaknesses by being open and free and later be forced to become overly defensive. So we would rather be more on the offensive toward others than always defending ourselves. We would rather be slightly offensive than slightly defensive in dealing with others than go too far one way or the other and get too upset in our interaction. For we don't like to be put on the defensive or offensive too much because of the fear of creating emotional tension in our lives. Getting rejected and in a bad light and not being able to continue interaction with others is not sought after because we know our emotions will suffer and we will feel depressed because of it.

What is a challenge and goal to one person might not be to another. You might have different abilities in some areas from someone else. Therefore, each person needs his or her own goals, or the emotions need solid goals in order to relax. Two people could be reaching the same goal, but one is relaxing and the other is not and might even become bored and indifferent by the same goal, so everyone's offensive goals have to be set up especially for their own distinct needs. If there's no striving, there's no releasing of one's tensions. Therefore, it's of the utmost importance for releasing of our own emotional tensions, a must for mental health and to develop good relationships. We always feel comfortable when we express our feelings completely, as the mind releases emotional enzymes, which make us feel good and relax our emotions. The mind's method to get us competitive is to make us satisfied and happy when we do as we should. So we must learn more about doing what we naturally should do to feel comfortable. For when our emotions are relaxed so are we, and since defensive feelings do not release emotional tensions we should stay away from resisting others, as these defensive feelings make us uncomfortable, since there is no reward created in our minds for defensive resistance. Everything in our mind is tied up to offensive competitive involvement, which releases our emotional tensions; therefore, we're primarily offensively oriented. Why do men climb mountains? Because of the challenge and the resistance the mountains provide. This is the same reason man gets involved in any sport or other activity, the competitive release. All our competitive involvement includes resistance of some form. But defensive action is an extremely important part of this and should not be overlooked. Also, the level of defensive resistance is really the key to successful competitive release, for too much resistance stops offensive competitive endeavors. Stopping someone's competitive action with too much resistance will put him or her into emotional turmoil and eventually depression. So, defensive resistance must not be to stop a person completely, but to support and guide him or her to try harder, for the harder a person tries, the more emotional release there is, which satisfies the mind and creates a more comfortable feeling, which we all desire. Searching out the proper resistance, therefore, becomes the sole aim of our emotions. Too much is no good, and too little is no good. How hard the resistance should be depends on each person's emotional levels. The harder the resistance, the more release of the emotions. This should be taken in account when dealing with depressed people. But if a person can't handle resistance very well because he or she is too weak, that person must start with lighter resistance, until he or she can handle more. For too much resistance for a weak person could stop him or her, causing more emotional turmoil. Therefore, the resistance must be suited to the person to be effective for his or her mind.

A lot of people with emotional problems blame them on things that happened in their youth or even later in life. In fact, almost everyone has had things happen to them in their past that could be called abuse and therefore caused emotional difficulties. Some people who experience the same abuse as others develop emotional problems while the others don't. We tend to blame bad things that have happened to us in the past for our current depressed feelings. A lot of these bad feelings are due to a lack of expressing and releasing our emotions normally. They build up because they are not being vented properly, so depression sets in. Some people who have had abusive things happen to them in the past are not troubled by these bad experiences and carry on a normal life. I feel this is due to the fact that their emotions are vented properly and therefore their problems modify and don't bother them. So you can see the advantage of learning how to release emotions to keep yourself from later developing a buildup of them, for your mind will look to any abuse or other bad thing that has happened to you in the past to blame for your current emotional tensions and depression because you're hurting, not realizing it's the emotional buildup in your mind that is the real cause of your difficulties. The mind must express its emotions to stay relaxed, but letting them build up and cause tension will create havoc and depression for the rest of your life. Any bad, hurtful event in your life that causes you to stop pursuing your goals can be a disaster for your emotions, so continue with other goals if at all possible.

The natural blending that takes place when defensive and offensive actions between people are occurring is very rapid and quite subtle and hidden most of the time. These quick changes when people switch from defensive to offensive tactics as they interact are often so subconscious and subtle that they are hard to follow. But when the conversation is analyzed afterward, one can see when offensive and defensive actions change to one or the other. The interaction is rapid and seems to blend defensive and offensive tactics, but by watching carefully you can see which person is being more offensive than the other or whether it's more mutual. Some people are more defensive than others and follow certain emotional thought patterns that help them remain defensive as they interact with others, and some people are highly offensive in their actions. These differences often make it possible for certain people to become friends by each providing what the other lacks emotionally. As you mature, some of your likes and dislikes change, often leading to changes in goals and pursuits, due to emotional changes taking place that need gratification.

Because man is competitively oriented emotionally, you can understand why abuse or other harsh treatment can be taken differently under similar circumstances and have totally opposite results. Two men could be in the same foxhole during a bitter battle and one of these men, because he had different emotional tensions, would become a mental case while the other, because his competitive nature was not stopped, fought hard, striving against his opponents, and would succeed in becoming a hardened veteran.

So many illustrations could be shown in which when the difficulties were too much to overcome they created emotional problems, but when the problems were overcome they did not. So abuse in the past could hurt one emotionally in a permanent way, but with support and solid encouragement toward new goals it could be kept under control. Never let some traumatic event stop you permanently. After a very short time look toward finding new goals in order to relax your emotions through competitive striving. The longer you're prevented from pursuing challenging goals, the harder it will be to get moving again. Start slowly on small goals, then increase your competitive efforts as best as you can. Often due to life's circumstances a person is forced emotionally into living a defensive existence. This type of life is much harder to live, because you're not expending your competitive energies as you should to relax your emotions. When you're forced into this type of lifestyle, you have to change your goals and how you pursue them, which is not easy to do. Goals that you once enjoyed you can no longer pursue due to the changing of your lifestyle by becoming more defensive, but you can't relax and do nothing or your emotions will build up and you'll become depressed. You must act. Remember, you have to find new goals or your emotions won't release the stimuli through your competitive strivings, the only method your mind uses to relax itself. Defensive efforts, unless closely associated with offensive strivings, won't help you relax, so don't remain defensive unless it's a means you're using to find offensive opportunities to pursue. As resistance is defensive in nature and if you're forced into this type of lifestyle, then you can't be offensively oriented. Understand that you won't be releasing your emotions and they will build up. So if you can change your lifestyle, then look for new goals to pursue that will take effort on your part to accomplish.

Most friendships are based on our emotional needs and the gratifying of them. We pick friends based on how we interact emotionally with them and understand how they express themselves in seeking to achieve goals. We evaluate people subconsciously and see if they will complement our own need for expression. If they do help us emotionally, this means either we will support them or they will support us. As we pursue goals, our friends help us by supplying what we lack and strengthening our efforts to achieve these goals. If we have more defensive or offensive feelings, due to our upbringing, we will pick the opposite person to complement us and help us modify our own efforts so we can realize our goals. If your feelings are too offensive or defensive you will have more difficulties achieving your goals, because many more people will reject your approach. So we modify our attitude toward other people by making friends who have opposite emotional feelings than we have. By teaming up with friends who have the opposite emotional approach to goals, then we are able to achieve what we weren't capable of achieving before. We like others because they complement us and help us accomplish our goals. We will feel uncomfortable subconsciously if we're too offensive or defensive and the rejection we get from others will make us want to modify our attitude and efforts. So we do this by teaming up with someone who has opposite emotional needs than we do and interacting with them, thereby relaxing our own emotions. As we interact with this special person, this is also competitive and helps us relax our emotions, allowing us to pursue more personal goals that we weren't able to pursue before this needed relationship was developed.

Most of our problems are caused by other noncompatible personalities with whom we come in contact. These involve emotional differences and conflicts between personalities. These hindrances and conflicts between our personalities are noncompatible for releasing our emotions in an offensive and striving way. Most of the interaction between people that is noncompatible and causes overly defensive or offensive emotional patterns to develop in the mind is caused by natural subconscious personality resistance. This resistance is toward efforts by others trying to get us to do things that we can't accept emotionally. We naturally won't, because of our particular competitive instincts to do it our way and subconscious desire to release our emotions a certain way, but this is done by expressing our emotions offensively in a positive manner. Any interference by others naturally makes us resist them, mostly in a subconscious way. All that we're aware of consciously is that we can't seem to agree to what they want. We even develop hidden emotional and subconscious methods resisting their efforts in order not to do what they want us to do. Since this is subconscious and we don't understand consciously why we're developing objective difficulties to what they're trying to get us to do, we tend to say, "It's because I don't like to do whatever I'm asked." But it's because of our own personality makeup and natural competitive nature to resist others, not any real dislike or resentment. Therefore, our natural competitive instincts always resist and offensively try to assert their own needs, because our emotions work off their energies better this way. When our personalities change, due to strong influences from other people and unusual circumstances coming into our lives, we tend to blame those around us, even though it's mainly the fault of our own different competitive natures being put into unusual defensive positions. Since we can't survive emotionally in overly defensive attitudes, as we don't release emotional energies this way, we try to move away from circumstances that we feel contribute to these situations. We feel if we change our environment we will get rid of our emotional difficulties, when they're really due to our not releasing our built-up emotions. As we find new goals we can strive after, our emotions will stabilize. Often strong feelings will dominate in our minds when we're depressed emotionally; these are survival-type emotions. These emotions are stronger and surface whenever we're not releasing emotional energies in our normal competitive methods. Since survival is paramount in nature, our self-preservation and sexual emotions become dominant and influence our lives more as we get depressed. So a society without strong goals can look ahead to more sexual and self-preservation feelings surfacing in the lifestyle of its people. You can understand that as man feels more insecure he will defend himself more aggressively from others, feeling he's threatened, and murder and suicide will increase. Sexual violence, due to stronger sexual emotions, also increases as these two emotions become more dominant. When normal emotions are depressed, these stronger emotions will always surface as nature tries to preserve itself.

When everyone is working toward similar goals or there's a major goal everyone is interested in trying to accomplish, there's overall harmony in the group. Whoever interferes or tries to stop striving after these goals is considered an enemy or unfriendly. This is the way we decide on friendship; our friends help us achieve success in our goals. Those that hinder or stop us from achieving our goals we view as unfriendly and even enemies. Sometimes someone will be trying to help us, but we're not sure and think that person is our enemy until we can see he or she is trying to help; then that person will become a friend. So it is very important to us to achieve our purposes and goals, for our mind stimulates and rewards us when we are successful in our pursuits. That's why we often are comforted by thoughts of our family, because we know our parents always helped us accomplish pursuits. If they didn't support us, we have a negative feeling toward them. Negative feelings are defensive and hinder the mind from striving after what it's trying to accomplish. Offensive feelings of the mind create good positive stimuli so as to get us to strive forward, as the mind has a way of rewarding itself when it is doing what is natural and normal. Defensive situations are always present and make us try all the more, and this is acceptable to our mind. Only when defensive situations stop us or hinder us too much does the mind start becoming alarmed, for our mind is programmed in a competitive-oriented way. Defensive or hindering elements in our lives must be viewed carefully so they don't stop us and we can continue striving after our goals, especially if they are of a beneficial nature. Often you can see how abuse and other hindrances could be viewed differently if taken as correction and making us achieve our goals; then it could be taken as a help instead of abuse. If you're driving down the road, laws governing your speed and stop signs don't hinder but help you get to where you're going. But if the laws hinder and stop you from proceeding to a destination, they become harmful; so it is with discipline and correction. If correction helps, it's okay and beneficial, but if it stops you, the discipline becomes harmful and is viewed the same way in our emotions. So at times what we would normally view as abuse is not; it's really how it affects our emotions by allowing them to express themselves that is considered beneficial. So don't let hindrances and abuse stop you; overcome them and proceed and you will become stronger, but if they stop you they will hurt you emotionally and will permanently hurt you if you don't continue.

Emotional events that take place today are categorized according to learned behavior patterns and similar events that happened in the past and how you dealt with them then, and you will handle them similarly. We take past emotional events that affected us in a somewhat similar fashion and use this data to judge something emotionally happening to us now. When you approach serious emotional events taking place in your life, plan out several ways that you might handle them; don't let them stop you emotionally. Plan how you can go ahead with your life as serious emotional things happen that you know you'll have trouble handling. So when something serious does happen it doesn't hurt you emotionally, but you can continue on a plan of action that will prevent you from being devastated. A sudden fearsome event will stop your emotions and is extremely dangerous to the functioning process of the mind. Don't let fear hurt you. Have plans you can implement when bad things happen, because fear can devastate and stop you unless you plan on what to do. Keep the emotions operating and don't let fear paralyze their functioning, because once they stop for a while it could be difficult getting them moving again.

We are placed on the defensive many times during the day as we interact with others. We can tell in our conscious minds when we've been put on the defensive by our feelings, which are up or down slightly. When on the offensive, we feel okay and good. The changing of our moods takes place all day, as we're on either the offense or defense as we go through life. So we learn to evaluate how to go about our daily living by the feeling we receive in our emotions, either positive or negative. No one likes bad emotional feelings, so we strive, if possible, after any worthwhile goal we can achieve, because we know if we're doing something we feel better. If there are no positive goals around, due to our environment, we will follow any competitive goal that we become aware of, because of the need to release our emotions. Because defensive and offensive feelings are so intertwined in our daily interactions, we don't interpret them knowingly; the only thing we're aware of is how we feel, good or bad, not how to evaluate them.

Remember also that in nature weakness and strengths are relative principles and always follow similar patterns. So competitive goals must be evaluated so that we follow patterns toward success and not toward failure.

Man must express himself to find fulfillment in life, and expression must meet resistance to reach its conclusion, for expression without resistance is nothing but emptiness. So man is competitive the only way he can fulfill this part of his emotional nature, which is by the need to express himself completely. Man also determines reality by the resistance he receives to his expression—a relationship the mind must have to operate sensibly.

There are natural laws that make all living things strive to succeed. All animals strive for leadership in their environment. The strongest and smartest make it; the weakest fall by the wayside. This striving in nature leads to a more efficient and successful environment. The weak fall by the wayside because the laws of nature do not allow them to survive; only those that strive will survive. Everyone is under those natural laws. Some among us strive and make it; some cannot. Their poor environment causes them to fail. So man must have the chance to strive for different goals, even in a poor environment, or he won't make it but will fall by the wayside. We must provide goals for everyone in our society. Not doing so condemns people, for we must strive in order to live. There are many illustrations in nature that could be used to show that those that strive live and those that don't will not. I think we're all aware of these examples in nature, such as a female deer in estrus, while attracting many males, only allowing the buck that is the most powerful stag to be her mate. In the wolf family, only the dominant female wolf in the pack is allowed to breed and then only with the dominant male of the pack, thus assuring the strongest and best pups will live. From nature we must realize we can't escape these natural laws, but we should conform to them. Whereas most of nature is limited in how they must strive and stay within their narrow environment, man is not. Man is not limited in his competitive striving but has a wider sphere, with more abilities in which to release these competitive energies than the rest of nature, but he still has to strive in order to live. Societies must find goals for all of their members if they want to survive under the laws of nature. There is no forgiveness in nature.

As ancient Rome fell due to internal weaknesses of turmoil, so will any society. A society is destroyed from within; the same with the individual. The individual is destroyed not, as he or she might think, by those blamed for his troubles, but by his or her own conflicting emotions. Built-up emotions will destroy a person internally unless he or she gets rid of them.

I wrote this book not only to describe man's natural competitive nature, as there are plenty of books written on competitiveness in business, sports, you name it, but because I want to illustrate how our emotions use this competitive system we have to relax our minds. Relaxation of emotional tensions is of the utmost importance for mental well-being. Through our competitive nature our interests and abilities, with the necessary emotional input, are expressed. That's why I wrote this book, to illustrate this emotional need of ours. You can try out this emotional experiment on yourself. See if you release your emotions by sitting on your duff or striving after competitive interests that you have. This experiment needs time to work, but sit around doing nothing for a few weeks, then start striving after goals that interest you, and notice the difference in your feelings. If you have emotional difficulties at this time, like something stressful happening to you when you're experimenting, you will notice you'll feel tension and anxiety start to build as you're resting and taking it easy. Then start striving after pursuits of one kind or another; you'll notice the difference. Even though our emotions do not utilize defensive situations to relax their tensions, it is, nonetheless, a vital part of our overall competitive release, so I illustrated this as well.

When we have tension or turmoil in our lives, this produces emotional buildup in our minds. This cannot remain in our minds or it will cause anxiety and depression. Rest and relaxation will not get rid of these tensions. Any therapist who says rest and relaxation will take care of this problem really doesn't understand that it won't go away by itself. Plenty of rest might help you live with problems, but it won't get rid of them, just help you bear them. Only through the mind's normal methods can these tensions disappear. I have often wondered why others haven't written about releasing competitive tensions through pursuits, for I know they're aware of this action. I waited for years, not writing about this because I thought more educated and smarter people could do a better job describing this competitive action. Since no one has approached this need, explaining how this information would be beneficial to understanding our emotions a little easier, I thought I would write and try to do this. There are many other thoughts I've mentioned in this book in passing that I did not explain, but maybe I'll write about some of these later.